PLANTS
— WITH —
IMPACT

John Kelly

English Rose 'The Pilgrim'

David & Charles

To my children
Tim, Chris and Clare

'And so she went to this doctor – it seems he examines you in regard to the way you react to color – he is what they call a Color Analyst.'

RUTH DRAPER,
Doctors and Diets

A DAVID & CHARLES BOOK

© John Kelly 1992

First published 1992
Reprinted 1993

ISBN 0 7153 9986 1

Typeset by ABM Typographics Ltd, Hull
and printed in Italy
by New Interlitho SpA
for David & Charles
Brunel House   Newton Abbot   Devon

CONTENTS

CHAPTER 1

—◦❧◦—

THE IMPACT OF PLANTS

—◦❧◦—

'Any color, so long as it's red, is the color that suits me best.'

EUGENE FIELD,
1850–1895

'Green bloomers? – Oh, no – green is a lovely shade. Any shade that is near to nature is dear to me.'

RUTH DRAPER,
A Class in Greek Poise

The fierce brightness of red and pink Michaelmas daisies is a delight, but one to be taken in short doses. If we had evolved on a red world, we might well find colours such as these the most restful of all

If we were members of a species that had evolved on a distant planet, where the sky was yellow and the ground was red, it is fairly certain that we would be so attuned to a red and yellow world that we would find it beautiful. It would be hard to survive otherwise.

We would find it restful to live with red and yellow as constant, day-long elements in our lives. Other colours – greens and blues, for example – would appear as passing ornaments, to be deployed with care lest they clashed, highly attractive for short spells, but tiring in the long term.

Our entire artistic culture would be based on the colours of our environment. There would be yellow skies over our country's cliffs, we would live in a red and pleasant land, and my love would be like a green, green rose.

As it is, our species evolved under blue skies and surrounded by green. Neutral greys and fawns appeared from time to time with the seasons and appeared pleasant enough, if sometimes vaguely depressing, and yellows and reds – tiring colours if looked at for too long – came and went in the shape of flowers and fruits, never staying for many days of the year's cycle.

For a non-reflective intelligence such as a horse or a monkey, evolution merely dictated that the world should be comfortable and relatively safe. As long as the horse had green under his feet there was plenty of food; moving patches of fawn suggested lions. For the monkey, green meant everything good in a monkey world, but for the brightness of certain delicious fruits.

Man, who thinks about the world, is furnished – perhaps burdened – with emotions. Life is not just a matter of getting by; he has to *feel* about it. For our ancestors, as for ourselves, green was physiologically the most restful colour, and therefore they felt good about it, needed it and, truth to tell, loved it. Other than that, blue was probably the colour that created the greatest feeling of calm. Ask any child what his favourite colour is; the chances are that it will be blue. The colours of emotions such as excitement, astonishment, anticipation and joy were bright yellows, reds, oranges, and so on.

Green is the backdrop against which other colours are measured. The red new leaves of the photinia draw the attention, but the brightly contrasting, variegated foliage nearby demands it much more. Always, however, the eye has the chance to return to green

Because Man is reflective, simply to feel these things is not enough. He has to ask 'Why?'. If a certain arrangement of trees gives him good feelings, he will analyse the cause and effect and come up with something like, 'It means home' or, 'There were some like that when I was a child'. He might even say, 'The arrangement is balanced and the flowers drape themselves nicely over the foliage'.

*Modern Man attempts to dispose plants in the way that satisfies him most. . . He imagines **he** orders and controls them, but in fact it is the other way round. It is their impact upon him that is the stronger force*

Looking tentatively ahead, as Huxley, Wells, and Arthur C. Clarke have done, it is possible to imagine yet another planet; one to which Man's reflective intelligence has led him. An artificial environment of concrete – or something like it – is all he knows. His brave new world is synthetic, angular, clad in neutral tones with patches of imperious colour. It is not difficult to imagine the discipline and amount of medication needed to contain the resulting emotions such as anxiety, restlessness, depression and irritability.

It is surely highly likely that the inhabitants of that future world would crave the company of green plants and long for the sight of a blue sky. Of course, it is also almost certain that they would have at least the former, since NASA is currently conducting experiments to find out how plants will grow in such artificial and probably low-gravity environments.

In our own time, we find ourselves somewhere in between. Few of us are lucky enough to live in a green and blue world and we mostly find ourselves spending our working days in rectangular rooms, the vast majority of which are decorated in tones from the grey and fawn range. On our way home we gaze at grey freeways and jumbles of vehicles whose colours constantly jazz and clash in a most unrestful way. We long for the restfulness of green, the calm of blue, and a harmonious disposition of the bright, short-term colours.

Our deep, atavistic desire to remain close to the natural world shows in the plants we bring into our workplaces and the difference it makes to us if our work building has a garden or is next to a park is enormous. A secretary who has a rubber plant by his or her desk and who can walk in Central Park or Kensington Gardens at lunch hour will be far happier as a result, and the boss's stress may well be alleviated if some plants are kept growing in his office.

Perhaps most of all, this yearning is manifest in gardening. Modern Man, ancient instincts modified by reflection, constantly asking 'Why?', attempts to dispose plants in the way that satisfies him most. His emotions, complicated and interreacting, and his aesthetic sense, which is arguably the extension of his emotions, are affected by the plants he chooses and then coaxes into making the kind of picture he seeks.

He imagines *he* orders and controls them, but in fact it is the other way round. It is their impact upon him that is the stronger force.

PLANTSMAN OR DESIGNER?

Once a gardener passes beyond the stage of being a beginner, he (hereinafter to be taken as including she) is almost certain to develop along one of three directions.

The Plantsman
The first, followed by those who find that they love plants for their own sake, is that of the plantsman. This is less a description one can apply to oneself than a title, only to be bestowed by others. You can say, 'He is a plantsman' but you cannot say, 'I am a plantsman'. It is bragging, as you do not set out to become one; it just happens.

(By the way, it should never be forgotten that the very best gardeners are and always have been women. The feminine of plantsman is also 'plantsman' but it is perfectly proper to refer to a plantswoman. However, let us please have no truck with 'plantsperson' or any other such expression of the neuter.)

A plantsman is someone whose love of plants is deep and abiding but who also knows a great deal about them. He will probably feel that the more he learns the less he knows, but that is right and

The gleam of a sunlit leaf, the poise and promise of a tender young shoot and a certain indefinable elegance are the sorts of qualities that appeal to the plantsman. A species rhododendron in an Irish garden

The almost legendary tree peony, *Paeonia suffruticosa* 'Joseph Rock' would be a desirable foliage plant even if its flowers were less sumptuous

proper, as several lifetimes would not be enough for a truly thorough knowledge of the plant world. The plantsman is fluent in the use of Latin names and may be positively learned in his own field, while often being anything but academic in other aspects of his life.

Plantsmen love plants. This means that they do not single out flowers for their enjoyment, but admire each plant as an entity. They will, for example, think much more of a species rose like *Rosa glauca* than of any modern Large-Flowered or Cluster-Flowered rose. To them, the foliage colour, stance and habit of the shrub and the balance between the plant and its flowers are far more desirable than the enormous, high-crowned blooms on the amorphous, annually decapitated bushes.

A plantsman can get quite excited about a plant whose flowering is erratic, as long as its other qualities attract him. Species rhododendrons, for example, which tend to have off-years and only to flower really well once every three or so, are greatly superior to the eye of a plantsman than the highly bred hybrids that bloom mightily every time. The impact they have on him is far greater. It is not that he actively disapproves of the hybrids; they just do nothing for him, whereas the species overwhelm him with their beauty *as plants*.

Plants impress themselves on a plantsman as individuals. Take a plantsman to the Himalayas, place him in a grove of the exquisite *Daphne bholua*, and watch his reactions. He will, of course, say 'Wow!' just like anyone else at first, but in no time you will find him poring over the minutiae of the plants, searching for differences, seeking out superior forms, and studying leaves as intently as flowers.

It is to plantsmen that we owe the presence of garden plants with beautiful features other than flowers, but we should never discount their appreciation of flowers as essential parts of the plants. They will ruthlessly reject a poor bloom, but are quite capable of changing that judgement if just such a flower occurs on a plant whose other characteristics are greatly superior.

Some people maintain that plantsmen are poor gardeners. This is not true. Plantsmen adore their plants and often go to great lengths to make them comfortable and 'at home'. They know a lot about gardening in terms of the needs of individual plants; what they lack, to a greater or lesser degree, is concern with the interplay of plants in making an aesthetically satisfying whole. To them each plant is satisfying, so the whole garden is, too.

The Flower Gardener

Something of the same thinking – if that is what it is; 'feeling' might be a better word – lies behind the way in which members of the second strand of gardeners operate. These are people for whom the flower is everything. The foliage must, of course be healthy and flourishing, but only in so far as it is the larder of the flowers.

Gardening is all about joy and pleasure, which are dictated by the plants. . . If you cannot please yourself in your own garden, where can you?

There are three different kinds of flower gardener. One consists of those for whom massed summer colour in the form of annuals brings the greatest joy. The desire for green is satisfied by lawn, while the stamina that a constant barrage of colour demands is reduced by this being a summer phenomenon only. You can see stunning gardens of summer colour in Ireland; some so joyously flamboyant that you find yourself laughing in astonished agreement. But then, there is a lot of green about in Ireland and you are never far away from it. The Irish can afford to paint their houses in outlandish colours that only they and their emerald country can get away with. In Killarney, for exam-

ple, there is a timber-frame building on which the woodwork is picked out in a blue made all the more royal by the local light. The little garden in front is entirely blue annuals, the lobelia matching the house exactly. It works – in a dazzling sort of way.

There is no question of the colour-mass gardener being remotely interested in the plants themselves. It is the flowers that are everything. Neither, though, is it the individual flower that engages his attention.

This can be said, too, of the lover of the monochrome border. Generally speaking there is a social divide between the planter of massed annuals and the owner of a yellow border or a blue garden, but their concerns are the same. It is the colour effect that is paramount. While the one will assert that the choice is governed by 'taste', the other will probably give not a fig for such a concept. Who, then, is right?

Well, neither is wrong, that is certain. Gardening is all about joy and pleasure, which are dictated by the plants – not social or artistic censure, which are inventions of Man. If you cannot please yourself in your own garden, where can you? However, the differences are there to see and there are lessons to be learned from them.

This kind of gardener tends to be the antithesis of the plantsman in that he – but it is more frequently she – will over-ride the interests of the individual plant in favour of attaining chromatic perfection. A plant that prefers shade is likely to be made to grow in full sun despite the knowledge that its life will be greatly shortened, just so that it can contribute to the colour scheme for a season or so.

Here foliage does play a part. One-colour beds often have a strong foliage component – shrubs with golden leaves and Bowles's golden grass in yellow borders, for example – but this does not alter the fact that this type of border is a result of flower gardening. The foliage is not there for its own sake but because it fits in with the exclusively golden flowers.

The white garden is the ultimate in monochrome. That it is extremely and often prohibitively labour-intensive is seldom pointed out, but if you do not dead-head constantly, you soon have a brown garden. Generally speaking, one-colour gardens are a horticultural dead-end and most of their advocates become tired of them. Those whose efforts become celebrated are often doomed to become the weariest of all. For a while, though, and for those who merely visit, they can provide enjoyable experiences of some sophistication.

The third kind of flower gardener is another sort of monoculturist, for whom the individual flower is the centre of horticultural existence. Experts in this field can be said to have brought great benefit to gardening; it can also be maintained that their works sometimes verge on the monstrous.

Enthusiasts, whether amateur or professional, for the modern rose, chrysanthemum, dahlia, camellia, begonia, carnation, and many more, derive much joy from their activities. If the flowers become over-large, over-double, top-heavy or of too violent a hue, should we complain? Yes, if it means the elimination from the world's flora of the original species. But if not, then it is surely foolhardy to denigrate activities that give some people such simple and harmless pleasure.

The Designer

The third gardening strand is made up of designers. These are people, basically artistic, on whom plants make an impact when pressed into the service of a design. They are different from the one-colour gardeners in that their plans take in all colours and combinations, but are similar in that the plants themselves come second to the effect achieved by the interaction of all the design elements.

Plants themselves vary greatly in their garden-worthiness. It would be fatuous and quite ignorant to erect an altar to the uncritical worship of plants

A fourth can, I suppose, be discerned: the vegetable gardeners. However, it can be argued that they too are susceptible to the impact of the individual plant. Certainly the biggest marrow, leek or onion is a plant with impact. We should watch this group with a constant learning eye; look at some of the finest potagers and you will find exquisitely designed gardens in which sympathetic treatment of the individual plant and plants en masse is combined with a feeling for the interactions of the plants and the use of plants as design elements.

It is just this combination of factors that fully recognises and exploits the impact that plants have on us. None of our gardening stereotypes sets out to become a disciple of the individual plant or of the massed colour effect. Each has, however, felt the primeval impact of plants deep in his spirit and followed it where it led. If we consciously lay ourselves open to the seductive qualities of the individual plant as well as to the effects of plants acting together; if we recognise that we live in a real world and allow the plants to combine harmoniously with our artefacts, and if we avoid the excesses of fashion and trendiness, we should begin to find ourselves once more at one with a green and blue, bejewelled world.

PLANTS WITH CHARACTER

However, we should not be too starry-eyed, either about gardening or about the natural world. Plantsmen can become too uncritical and start to become besotted by weeds, green flowers and rarity for its own sake. Flower gardeners all too readily forsake common sense when the vase beckons, and such things as wooden roses, hideous, unfixed variegations and luridly dyed blooms take centre stage.

Plants themselves vary greatly in their garden-worthiness. It would be fatuous and quite ignorant to erect an altar to the uncritial worship of plants. The world is full of plants that are poisonous and evil-smelling, armed with vicious thorns or leaves sharper than any spear, or simply ugly. There are plants that look well in their native haunts but unprepossessing in captivity, others whose flowers last but a day, and many more that are just not all that attractive.

What we must not forget is that our gardens are very small indeed. If we take all the plants that are hardy enough to grow out of doors and then eliminate those with the undesirable characteristics above, and after that rule out all but the most attractive, we should still be faced with a bewildering array, infinitely too large for any garden.

We can enjoy plants on quite a wide scale by visiting other people's gardens. In fact, it is arguably the best way of learning. However, when it comes down to what we are to grow ourselves, we face a very narrow choice from the material that is available.

The Scotch thistle. Beauty or beast?

Knowing that plants affect us more than we realise, should we not maximise their effectiveness? If so, then we should learn to look for the characteristics that give a plant influence and enchantment and make it impressive, imposing, or charming. If possible, each plant should have more than one salient feature, although we will have to allow for those whose one main attribute is so powerful that it rightfully demands space.

It is not enough to judge a plant's qualities by what it looks like in the garden centre or nursery bed – although you can tell readily enough if it has been badly looked after. Neither should you rely on catalogue descriptions. A young plant cannot possibly demonstrate all the qualities of the adult, and nursery descriptions, no matter how honest, are short (because of economics) and designed to sell the product.

There is really no alternative to a little research and study. The best research involves seeking out mature specimens in gardens, particularly large gardens that are open to the public, and study need mean no more than a visit to the local library.

Suppose, for example, you were to find a 1.2m (4ft) specimen of *Liquidambar styraciflua* for sale in a garden centre. What information you would be given would be certain to emphasise the autumn colour of this maple-like tree, as it changes early and becomes vivid red in the right conditions. What you would be unlikely to be told is that it grows to 18m (60ft) in England and 45m (150ft) in eastern parts of North America. That it does nothing else for the rest of the year except to be green in spring

Persicaria vacciniifolia (syn *Polygonum vacciniifolium*) in autumn. The foliage of this rock plant is quite attractive during spring and summer, and it flowers well in late summer – but it is, after all, only a dock

and summer and bare in winter is hardly promotional material. You might still be likely to buy it if your thinking was simply, 'Oh yes, just the thing! I wanted some autumn colour'.

But it would be much better to be less impulsive and to research this particular aspect. Your approach can be from one of two directions. You can look at plants in gardens and then look them up to see what they do in autumn and, most importantly, what else they do; or you can go to the library first and look up autumn colour.

Of course you, being a wise gardener with foresight, have purchased or borrowed (I hope the former) this book, which has a gazatteer of plants. You will see that some have been marked as possessing good autumn colour, and a glance at the other information should tell you how much value you should attribute to a given plant. Deciduous azaleas, for example, put on a riotous show of dazzling colour in autumn, but are equally dashing in spring, when their flamboyant trumpets blaze out in a brilliance of tonal splendour.

After you have pursued your enquiries into the merits of several likely candidates for your autumn-colour spot, consulted books and gardening magazines and perhaps waited a year until you could see them planted elsewhere, it is more than probable that the liquidambar will be left for someone who wants to furnish a very large garden, even a demi-park. Meanwhile you will have marched gleefully off with a first-class rent payer like *Acer palmatum* 'Senkaki', whose display of canary-yellow autumn leaves precedes months of coral branchlets, brightly leafless against the stark winter light.

Words like research and study sound a little heavy, but in gardening they imply great fun. Few gardeners dislike reading about the subject, and I know of none who do not enjoy visiting gardens

Words like research and study sound a little heavy, but in gardening they imply great fun. Few gardeners dislike reading about the subject, and I know of none who do not enjoy visiting gardens. Looking at and looking up plants are essential to making a good choice. What you are assessing is two kinds of characteristics of plants, the tangible and the intangible.

TANGIBLE CHARACTERISTICS

You might at first think that the distinction between the physical aspects of a plant and those that are due to something less easily defined would be an obvious one. You might also think that the former would be much more important than the latter in determining the garden-worthiness of a plant. In both instances you would be mistaken.

Crocosmias are perennials that flower in late summer. They have iris-like foliage and brilliant, star-trumpet flowers in shades of red, orange and yellow. They are also known as montbretias. Almost all the ones that are grown are hybrids, and two species occur in the parentage of the vast majority, *C. aurea* and *C. masonorum*. Apart from variations in colour, the hybrids fall into two dis-

Crocosmia 'Lucifer', perhaps the most daring of the hybrids with upright flowers

tinct groups; those with nodding flowers, influenced by *C. aurea*, and those in which the flowers stand erect along the tops of the arching stems and take after the second species. These are tangible characteristics, easily seen and described in factual terms. That the hybrids with nodding flowers are rather tender by comparison with the upright ones (US zones 7-9) is tangible enough when they fail to come up after the first winter.

Unless you have some idea of the intangible qualities of plants, how can you possibly plant them to the best advantage?

What no catalogue or nursery blurb can tell you is the great difference in appearance, poise and character between the groups, or the entirely distinct message that each projects – in short, its impact.

Crocosmias with nodding flowers, no matter how brightly coloured, have a modest, natural appearance that makes them ideal for massing on banks or for growing, as they will perfectly well, among long grass. They are, for all their near-gaudiness, surprisingly restful and easy-going. On the other hand, those with upright flowers have a cocky, look-at-me air. They are daring plants, flaunting their brazen hues cockscomb fashion and brooking no challenge from ambitious lesser lights. On a grassy bank they would look like aldermen at a gypsy wedding; their place is in a broad border, treated with the deference due to their imperious carriage.

Crocosmias with nodding flowers multiply rapidly in mild climates and sometimes escape into roadside banks and hedge-bottoms. Nobody really minds. That the upright ones should do so is unthinkable; important – even self-important – dignitaries never form crowds and they certainly do not run wild!

The nurseryman who described plants in such a fashion would soon go out of business, a martyr to the cost of his catalogue, because you cannot describe intangible qualities in factual language. But unless you have some idea of the intangible

qualities of plants how can you possibly plant them to the best advantage? Nevertheless we must keep up the distinction between the tangible and intangible qualities of plants, otherwise we cannot discuss them coherently. What we should do, though, is to remember the lesson of the crocosmias when considering the purely factual aspects of plants.

Flower Power

Out of all these aspects, the greatest impression is made, in general, by flowers. Oh, there is an argument there all right: many would champion foliage as the leader in the virtuosity stakes, but gardeners as a whole love flowers and you only have to read the writings of plantsmen like Reginald Farrer and Frank Kingdon-Ward to know how often it was flower colour that beckoned them from across a valley or stunned them with brightly painted hillsides. Once among the plants, they would be captivated by the minutiae of form, but their 'Old Adam' eye leapt at colour, not habit.

We must never lose sight of the fact that flowers are brightly coloured specifically to attract attention. Their sole purpose is to become pollinated, not specifically to gladden the heart of man. So irrelevant are we to this purpose that many plants have flowers which, to us, are quite dowdy but which are ecstatically enticing to an insect that can see ultra-violet. Most pollinators, however, make a bee-line, as it were, for the same colours that we can see.

Once they have fulfilled their function the coloured, seductive petals are no longer needed and the inexorable logic of nature dumps them in favour of the developing seed. In the natural world our forebears did not need to evolve with an accommodation to bright colours except in the very short term, so we are not bound physiologically to them in the same way as we are to blue and green. Nonetheless we need them, but only in short bursts. We have always been able to look away from bright colours or to entertain them happily for short periods – unlike green and blue, to whose long-term presence we had to adapt or die. This enables us to be quite swingeing in our judgements of bright colour and to vary greatly one from the other in what colours we like, whether singly or in combination.

This is a matter of personal preference. To

It is a lesson in humility to realise that the flowers of *Gazania splendens* evolved not for our pleasure, but as bribes to insects that might pollinate them

illustrate this, I must become personal for a moment and recount my first realisation of the deeply primitive interplay that exists between flower colours and the brain. One day in the garden of a fellow horticultural writer, the late David Pople, I found myself staring fixedly into a clump of Californian poppies (eschscholzias) whose wide, single blooms were of a piercing, dazzling orange that was somehow at the same time cleansing and quietly pure. I found afterwards that a particularly pressing problem had fitted itself back into its proper proportion and no longer bothered me unduly. I have loved these flowers ever since and sow them whenever I can.

At the time I was head gardener to a young woman whose extremely broad acres included a large garden that was open to the public. She hated orange with an undisguised loathing and ordered me to remove some magnificent, six-foot, deciduous azaleas in whose flowers were the very distillation of all that is fierce and bright in orange. I did not refuse; neither did I comply. I understood, but could not bring myself to destroy such loveliness.

She may well have thought me possessed of appalling taste. Indeed she may have been right in general, but this was not a matter of taste. Taste is a cultural matter, capable of changing dramatically in a short period. It has a large element in it of fashion and of peer-group acceptance. Our opposite reactions to the orange flowers went far deeper than the dictates of civilisation and had their roots in heredity. Neither was right, nor wrong.

Should anyone doubt the fundamental impact that plants have on us, he need look no further than flowers for his doubt to vanish

Should anyone doubt the fundamental impact that plants have on us, he need look no further than flowers for his doubt to vanish. This *force majeure* that is brought to bear on us, when understood, transcends such considerations as, 'What will the neighbours think?'. The inner freedom to do as we please on our own land is a great prize that opens the gate to untrammelled pleasure.

However, it would be equally short-sighted to dismiss taste as to be governed by it. Having said that man is a reflective animal, constantly asking 'Why?', we should recognise that he also wants to know 'How?', the specific question in this case being, 'How do I create beauty?'

One immediate answer to someone whose primitive self is like that of my former employer would be 'Not with orange, that's for sure!' Fair enough. But what should the positive side of the answer be influenced by?

What pleases us in flower colours, shapes and styles, and what we perceive as beautiful in their combinations, is determined by two separate parts of our minds – if not two distinct compartments of the brain, one much older in evolutionary terms than the other. Each part, if we are to enjoy and use flowers as much as possible, needs to be open and receptive.

The first is the 'Old Adam' sector of our being, of which enough has been said. The other is the 'Modern Citizen'. This is the part of us that is subject to the influences that occur from the time we are born and that determine whether, for example, we think mauve to be romantic or redolent of our great-grandmothers. Those who went to finishing schools are liable to consider pastels the ultimate in good taste, while others, influenced perhaps by post-impressionist history of art classes at school, delight in 'pure' colour, unsullied by the addition of white. Some, taught that nasturtiums and petunias are vulgar, grow only lobelia and godetias; still others – in Bavaria, perhaps – delight in the nasturtiums that curl over their outer stairs and in the football-rosette petunias in the window-boxes below.

Given the infinity of combinations of primitive instincts and acquired preferences, it is unsurprising that so many different 'tastes' abound. It is surely also apparent that taste is neither 'good' nor 'bad', but just individual. If we can accept those influences that have affected our lives, recognise that our deepest and therefore most honest preferences are parts of our true selves, and then happily follow where each leads, we shall be allowing the influences of nature and civilisation to combine while neither dominates unduly.

Foliage Virtuosity

Sam Goldwyn said once, 'What we need are some brand new clichés'. Applied to gardening, his oxymoron was spot on: what could be more boring than the endlessly repeated 'Flowers come and go but foliage is always with us'? Unfortunately, clichés are almost always true. Still, it would be nice to give the late Mr Goldwyn his wish, so perhaps we may coin the dictum that foliage is the foundation of the garden, then turn it into a cliché by repeating it.

Foliage *is* the foundation of the garden. However, while that is as true as any other cliché, we should be constantly wary of the trap into which so many experienced gardeners fall – that of coming to believe that foliage is the be-all and the end-all, the sum total of the worth of gardening. One of Sam's other pearls was to the effect that a wide screen just makes a bad film twice as bad, and it is true that the bigger the garden, the more stultifying an over-emphasis on foliage becomes. It is, unfortunately, a fault most common among those with larger gardens, just as the obliteration of leaves by flowers occurs most commonly in smaller ones.

This is not to deny the fascination of an arboretum, as there you will find beauty of form as well as of

A happy relationship with foliage is based on an appreciation of its virtuosity. The colour green is like that theme of Paganini's on which all students are encouraged to write their own variations

foliage, which creates a different proposition altogether. What can lie in wait for us is a descent into an obsession with foliage – a fascination with the lurid and peculiar, a dark pursuit of strange variegations, and a driven search for the weirder things that can happen to leaves.

A happy relationship with foliage is based on an appreciation of its virtuosity. The colour green is like that theme of Paganini's on which all students are encouraged to write their own variations, occasionally with internationally renowned success. Other pigments should be like grace notes, never sonorous semibreves, and only a horticultural Beethoven should try his hand at introducing the darker ones as secondary themes. Green, in its many shades and moods, can be the subject of a

Foliage shape, as well as colour, can create stunning contrasts while helping to determine the mood of the garden. In this bold but appropriate planting, the blue-grey of *Hosta sieboldii* compares dramatically with the gold of the grass, *Hakonechloa macra* 'Albo-aurea'

(Opposite) The soft glow of a pieris in the full splendour of its rosy spring foliage is irresistible. The fact that it is evergreen, its generous flowering, and its 'quality' make it a shrub with universal appeal and not merely the plaything of collectors of coloured foliage

sonata, a symphony or a dance; it can display its virtuosity in the smallest garden as well as in a park.

The use of different shades of green can bring out the shapes and structures of adjacent plants which, if of similar shades, would be lost. For example, a holly, clipped into the shape of a globe, lacks drama if seen against an evergreen oak such as *Quercus ilex*, whose dark green is similar. However, a background of *Chamaecyparis lawsoniana* 'Pembury Blue' lends its shape a quiet and delightful emphasis, and a golden conifer such as *C.l.* 'Lane' throws it into sharp relief.

We should never lose sight of the impact of green foliage. It is the backdrop against which flowers come on stage, play their parts, and leave, but in the well-made garden it is capable of standing on its own. That it should never have to should now go without saying.

Leaf shape and size are tangible plant characteristics that have profound influences on gardens. A garden with a host of tall, spiky-leaved plants like phormiums, yuccas and large grasses will have a mediterranean look even though everything in it is hardy. Another, populated with large, broad-leaved plants like *Gunnera manicata*, ornamental rhubarbs and lysichitons, can hardly avoid being jungly. It is at this point that further consideration of foliage leads us into the realms of the intangible, where moods and emotions begin to be affected by the leafy world that once was home.

The Effect of Form

However, there is more to the tangible side of plants than flowers and foliage. Form, which is, in general terms, the shape and habit of plants, is very important indeed. If you choose a columnar tree over a globular one or prefer a horizontally branched shrub to one with a weeping habit, that particular plant's shape will exert a profoundly different effect on the garden. In purely physical terms it will be an architectural one, but we can quickly see how there would be a strong intangible impact as well.

Form can be used to great effect in complementing the shapes of buildings. A tall, thin house will be helped if the garden has some prominent specimens of wide, flat-topped junipers like *Juniperus sabina* 'Tamarascifolia' and prostrate ones such as *J. horizontalis* 'Bar Harbor'. A squared-off house is complemented by rounded shapes, and long, straight walls find counterpoint in upright shapes like *Sorbus* 'Joseph Rock' and *Chamaecyparis lawsoniana* 'Ellwoodii'.

We seldom stop to analyse the 'wow' factor in plants. If we are sufficiently impressed we just say, 'Wow!' and do not think much about it. Still, something must govern the immediate impact of a plant and it is highly likely, in a great many cases, to be its

To describe the new leaves of a rhododendron, lit by the sun of an early summer afternoon, is not a difficult task. The atmosphere they create, however, is more easily felt than put into words

shape. It may be, too, that shape can be a turn-off. Many people like the pencil-thin conifer *Juniperus virginiana* 'Skyrocket' and find such a vegetable screech-mark desirable. Others loathe it, consider it unnatural, and feel like reaching for the axe.

'Habit' is a word that combines the tangible with the intangible. It has to do with such nebulous qualities as gracefulness as well as with factual ones like

This is really where you have to allow the impact of a plant to work on you, so that you just say 'Wow!' and put it on your list

the possession of weeping branches. It is more a plantsman's word than one used by designers or flower enthusiasts, and we had better leave it for now to become clearer as we look at more plants.

There are still many other physical attributes of plants that we find alluring, dramatic or enchanting. Coloured bark, for example, is an often overlooked element that should figure largely in our choice of plants. Fruit, berries, seed pods, buds – all sorts of lesser attributes come into play and many of them greatly extend the season in one species or variety more than in another.

INTANGIBLE ASPECTS

What we are really discussing is what makes us choose the 'right' plants for our individual gardens. So far we should have come to an appreciation of the ways in which we are affected by the physical characteristics of plants and can perhaps understand a little better what motivates our choice.

When it comes to the intangible things about plants that make us like or dislike them, it becomes much harder to analyse and easier to be woolly. However, it may be that a certain woolliness is inevitable when you start to talk about 'presence', 'grace', and so on. And yet these qualities are, by and large, what set good plants apart from less desirable ones. They are most important, but our judgements of them can only be subjective. This is really where you have to allow the impact of a plant

to work on you so that you just say, 'Wow!' and put it on your list.

People with plantsmanlike tendencies often describe a plant as being 'good'. When they mention a 'good plant', what they mean is that, yes, its leaves, flowers, habit and form are excellent, but there is something extra, something that, for the moment, defies description. The plant has quality.

Qualities that Count

It is often difficult to put into words what it is about a plant that, all of a moment, enthrals us. There is, for example, a specimen of *Prunus subhirtella* 'Pendula' at the Royal Horticultural Society's garden at Wisley, set by a flight of steps. Its presence when in flower is arresting. It is not enough to say that its airy cloud of small, pink flowers is delicate but imposing; and it is only a partial explanation to point out its elegant, weeping habit. Some part of its impact is due to the setting, but what really has a profound effect is a quality of presence. 'Charisma' should not be a word that applies to plants, but it does.

There is no doubt at all that this tree is a 'good plant'. Take, as a contrast, *Prunus* 'Kanzan'. This

Glaucidium palmatum **is one of the most sought after of all plants for a humusy, moist soil in part shade. Its attraction derives not just from its large, lobed leaves and cool, poppy-like flowers, but from indefinable assets that can only be summed up in such terms as 'character' and 'quality'. The plantsman's accolade – 'a good plant' – is an understatement in this case**

ubiquitous street cherry with brazen, magenta-pink flowers, double in an over-ruched way that reminds one of dubious bars and neon strips lining the way from the docks, becomes even more vulgar when the blossoms, milk spilt in cheap port, clash stridently with the copper-bronze of its new leaves. Its branches are coarsely akimbo and the adult foliage is banal. This much accounts for facts. Beyond it, however, is a sheer tooth-grating nastiness that cannot be quantified. Thank heaven some people like it; it is not good to think of anything being totally unloved.

We must simply accept that plants may be elegant, graceful, majestic or piquant, and that many are common, vulgar, or just somehow lacking in quality

Sometimes – not least here – you will read of plants 'creating' atmosphere or 'engendering' an air of mystery, romance, gaiety, and so on. The rational mind will deny this possibility and dismiss it as silly. Nevertheless, plants really do these things. What is actually happening, of course, is that we are responding to associations that their presence suggests – the 'mediterranean' ambience 'created' by yuccas and agapanthus can only be recognised by those who know one when they feel it. Things that are 'Christmassy' or 'just like Corfu' are only so in the eyes of those who have experienced Christmas or been to Corfu. Even then, Christmas evoked by the baubles on a Norway spruce is not the same as that enshrined in the brilliant crimson flowers of *Metrosideros excelsa*, the superb, midsummer flowering New Zealand Christmas Tree.

We must simply accept that plants may be elegant, graceful, majestic or piquant, and that many are common, vulgar, or just somehow lacking in quality. However, the question continually arises – how on earth do I choose plants when these characteristics are not visible in the nursery row?

We already know the answer, but it is worth repeating. There is no substitute for getting to know plants in garden settings. This does not necessarily mean in gardens – you may learn more about *Ginkgo biloba* in the streets of Washington DC than

at Dumbarton Oaks – but it does mean actively going looking at plants on every available occasion.

THE FUGITIVE ALLURE OF SCENT

Our sense of smell is unlike any other sense. It is incredibly sensitive, yet quickly dulled. Scents are almost impossible to recall, yet their associations flood back compellingly when they are encountered again, no matter how much time has gone by. They are notoriously difficult to describe.

Scents are both tangible and intangible. 'Mmm! smell that!' is a reaction to a tangible stimulus, yet where is the scent? What is it? In what words would you distinguish it from another?

Writers on flowering plants and wine suffer the same paucity of vocabulary and, notably in the latter case, resort to similes. Pouilly Fumé is 'flinty', Loire reds are 'raspberry-scented', and burgundies run the whole gamut of soft fruit from blackcurrants to strawberries. None of these is an adequate description. Sometimes a flower really does carry the scent of something else – *Iris graminea* of greengages, for example, or *Cytisus battandieri* of pineapple. But what do greengages and pineapples smell of – irises and Moroccan brooms?

If the aroma of roast beef usually brings you rushing in from mowing the lawn, try for a moment to recall its smell. Don't just remember the effect the smell had – endeavour to re-live the exact olfactory experience. As we used to say in the playground, bet you can't.

Immersed one day in David Austin's garden, where the English roses were and are raised, I was surrounded by a heady mixture of fragrances that, even so, had a light and gentle touch. I walked with the great man in his rose field and judged meekly for myself, quietly sniffing here and there as we passed. I remember and cherish the experience as a highlight of my gardening life, yet I cannot really remember what a rose actually smells like until the next time I do so, even though I seem able to relive that day in every detail.

When you read of a plant that it has 'a fine perfume' or 'a sweet, fresh fragrance', you may take it that the author has probably experienced it. You should not, however, push him beyond his honest endeavour to express it in words, as scent is, for all its power and palpability, the ultimate intangible.

CHAPTER 2

PLANTS IN CO-OPERATION

'In painting, the most brilliant colours, spread at random and without design, will give far less pleasure than the simplest outline . . .'

ARISTOTLE

The most telling plant combinations are simple ones, in which each plant appears more arresting than it would have done on its own. *Rosa wichuriana* and delphiniums

The plantsman and the plant collector are likely to be fine gardeners in that they know all about finding the best places for their treasures to grow. What they will almost certainly not be is good garden makers. The Buddhist monk with his rake, making endless patterns in the sand round a few carefully placed rocks and just one gnarled old tree, is likely to be better at it than they are.

On the other hand, the designer who has nothing of the plantsman in him may produce pretty pictures in his garden, but they will never overcome the soullessness that results from lack of appreciation of the true beauty of plants. Only when the designer has opened his mind to the witchery of individual plants can he get them to co-operate with him in making a garden with real enchantment.

Schumann once said that in order to compose, all you had to do was remember a tune nobody else had thought of. For a garden to have impact it must be original. Your own ideas will always appear far more interesting than those that came to you from a manual of garden design. You can go to Ghent, or Chelsea or Atlanta, Georgia, and come away from their great flower shows with all sorts of thoughts, but they must be allowed to develop into elements of your own design, not one you have bought off the shelf.

Of course, if you already have or have developed a plantsmanlike turn of mind, the plants will have wreaked their will on you and you will already have

Good garden design is based on the premise that plants should be encouraged to co-operate so that their combined beauty is greater than the sum of their individual beauties

determined that certain of them are going to be in your garden, come what may. However, because you are a complete gardener – a garden maker – the Modern Citizen part of your mind is already engaged in seeking combinations of beautiful plants that will enhance their beauty.

Good garden design is based on the premise that plants should be encouraged to co-operate so that their combined beauty is greater than the sum of their individual beauties. This sounds grand, but it

Messages. The fuchsia flowers are enhanced by contrast with the artemisia's grey foliage, which is itself made to seem even more finely filigreed when seen against the fuchsia's rounded, green leaves

only means that the way you put the plants together is better than any haphazard arrangement. If you can't imagine it could be worse, think again, because some deliberate plantings are just awful.

Not so long ago a cartoon appeared in a newspaper, showing the back of an automobile. On it was the make, and then a whole series of letters, most of which were Zs and Xs with the odd 'i' and, of course, plenty of GTs, GLs, and so on. The caption read, 'Mine goes faster than yours'. Inanimate objects can transmit messages.

When you are planting, it is helpful to imagine what messages your plants are transmitting to one another and to you. For example, one blue campanula in a wide drift of white ones is saying, 'Look how white my neighbours are'. The glossy, deep-apple-green leaves of a hart's tongue fern beneath *Elaeagnus pungens* 'Maculata' are saying, 'See how bright the gold variegation above us is, and notice, please, that our fronds appear even more shiny next to foliage with a matt surface'.

If you plant a weeping tree next to one of severely upright habit, there is a marked contrast, but it is not just that each draws attention to the other. What happens is that messages such as, 'I am much more upright by comparision to this weeping tree than I would be if you saw me on my own', are generated.

If you want to avoid the pitfalls that lie in wait for all of us when we are garden making, it will help if you continually ask yourself what message the plants are going to transmit. You should be able to hear the shrieks emitted when the roses 'Super Star' (intense vermilion) and 'Fragrant Cloud' (dusky scarlet) are threatened with having to live alongside one another, and you may well suspect a murmur of, 'So what?', next time you set out to refurbish your all-yellow bed.

RELATED PLANTING

If a garden is notable for the absence of loud colour clashes and naggingly tiring expanses of the same tonal range, if the shapes and sizes of the plants complement one another, and if the contrasts and comparisons are peaceful, it will begin to be a harmonious garden.

Harmony is a fitting together of parts so as to form a connected whole. 'Connected' is the key word in this dictionary definition, especially where it applies to the harmony of a garden. One should not forget the house, the various parts or departments of the garden and the utilities such as paths; all these must be integrated into the whole, but where connections come in it is, above all, the plants that provide them.

That is not to say that they are merely links, although that is one of their functions. The roses on a pergola may well do a fine job in linking the lawn to the herb garden, but the sorts of connections that really make for harmony are those between plants. If they are right, the linkage of house to garden and one area to another becomes much more fluent.

Making connections between plants is not a new idea, but basing the garden design on them is. The term that best describes this principle is 'related planting.' Related planting is not yet another rigid, crackpot notion. It is infinitely flexible and allows all other design considerations to have their say. It just means that *whichever way you look in the garden the plants will be in harmony with one another.*

It is based on a plantsmanlike appreciation and use of all the good characteristics of plants, from the colours and styles of flowers to the colours and textures of twigs, branches and trunks. It takes account

Related planting. The foliage colour of the Japanese maple (*Acer palmatum* 'Dissectum Atropurpureum') is echoed beyond the temple by the similarly coloured young foliage of a photinia. Another maple, to the left, picks up the maple-leaf theme and translates it into green

of form and foliage and it constantly concerns itself with the intangible qualities of plants.

Related planting has to do with synergy – the creation of effects greater than the sum of the parts – while at the same time pointing up the qualities of outstanding individuals. It is essentially extremely simple and is readily applied if you remember the superficially silly notion whereby plants generate messages.

Rhapsody in Gold

It works like this. Take two 'messages' – ferniness and the colour yellow (gold) – and think about weaving them harmoniously into the fabric of a garden, any garden. Be prepared for other messages to suggest themselves as you develop your design, and start with a plant that combines the two mentioned above – say *Robinia pseudoacacia* 'Frisia'.

This is a well-known small tree that is grown for its striking pinnate (ferny) foliage, which is gold from when the leaves unfurl until they drop. It seldom flowers.

It needs to be planted where its presence will be telling but not strident. For example, it looks dreadful with a brick wall behind it and is wasted in front of the muddle of shapes and tones of a house. In the garden plan below it has a background of green trees thoughtfully provided by the neighbours.

At the opposite end of the garden is another quite small tree, again with golden foliage and fernily pinnate leaves. This is *Gleditsia triacanthos* 'Sunburst', whose leaves are light yellow in spring and become appley-greeny-gold in summer.

These two have much in common, although a contrast is provided between the robinia's loosely cylindrical shape and the rather more umbrella-like dome of the gleditsia. Putting them at this distance from one another provides two foci of greenness and goldness, but without there being too much of a good thing in one quick eyeful.

Mid-way along the broad border that lies to the right of the lawn is a specimen of the conifer *Juniperus* × *media* 'Old Gold'. This medium-sized juniper is wide rather than high and has branches that rise quite sharply but with a feathery droop at the tips. This forms a link between the two trees and creates a thread of gold along the angled border of the lawn. It also provides a permanent gold focus, as it keeps its colour throughout the year.

Across the lawn, a balance is struck by the

Trees (green) in neighbouring garden

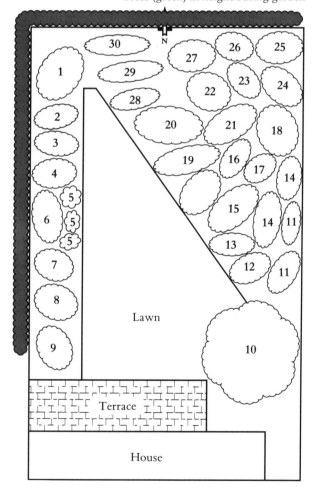

Related planting

1 *Robinia pseudoacacia* 'Frisia'
2 *Primula bulleyana* hybrids and yellow hemerocallis
3 *Meconopsis betonicifolia* and green hostas 4 *Acer palmatum* 'Atropurpureum'
5 *Rhododendron* 'Bow Bells'
6 *Camellia* × *williamsii* 'St Ewe' 7 *Weigela* 'Looymansii Aurea' 8 6 *Asplenium scolopendrium* 9 Gallica roses
10 *Gleditsia triacanthos* 'Sunburst' 11 *Hydrangea* 'Madame E. Mouillière'
12 *Primula pulverulenta*
13 2 *Rosa glauca*
14 *Hydrangea* 'Blue Wave'
15 6 *Polystichum setiferum*
16 *Juniperus* × media 'Old

Gold' 17 *Chamaecyparis* 'Pembury Blue'
18 *Rhododendron* 'Lord Roberts' 19 *Hemerocallis* 'Golden Chimes'
20 *Rhododendron* 'Humming Bird' 21 *Camellia japonica* 'Lady Clare' 22 *Acer palmatum* 'Senkaki' 23 *Pieris*
24 *Betula utilis jacquemontii*
25 *Acer griseum* 26 *Betula albo-sinensis* 'Septentrionalis'
27 *Acer negundo* 'Flamingo'
28 Variegated hostas
29 *Primula bulleyana* hybrids and yellow hemerocallis
30 Various meconopsis and primulas

presence of *Weigela* 'Looymansii Aurea'. This superb weigela has foliage of true gold that holds its colour until leaf fall and is bedecked with pink, foxglove-like flowers in summer.

Returning to the juniper, one finds beside it the taller, more or less conical *Chamaecyparis lawsoniana* 'Pembury Blue'. This has foliage that is steely blue and feathery-ferny in a different way from either the juniper or the two golden-leafed trees. On the northern side of the two conifers is a group of six of the soft shield fern, *Polystichum setiferum* – not one of the multiply divided varieties, just the plain, elegant species, whose fronds project as explicit a message of ferniness as it is possible to imagine. Here they will receive the partial shade and shelter from wind that they need.

Next to them is another group of ferns, this time the glossy, undivided, strap-shaped fronds of the hart's tongue, *Asplenium scolopendrium*. They pick up the fern theme but translate it into terms of shininess and undivided shapes. Another group is planted to the north of the weigela across the lawn.

Beyond the first group, and taking up the newly introduced theme of strap-shaped leaves, comes a wide band of *Hemerocallis* 'Golden Chimes'. This is a day-lily with a natural look; its relatively small flowers lack the near-formality of those with larger, broader petals, and it sits well with the wildness of the fern. It also picks up the gold theme directly from the juniper and reinforces it, while giving it an emphasis distinct from that of the trees and shrubs. Behind it – this is a lime-free garden with a rich, leafy soil – a shiny-leaved camellia takes the baton from the glossy hart's tongue and introduces a floral theme based on the owner's liking of informal blooms and firm, but manageable colours. It is *C. japonica* 'Lady Clare', whose large, semi-double, slightly floppy flowers suit the ambience of this garden, in which the daemon of the woodland rules, rather than the spirit of a sun-soaked, herby maquis.

Across the lawn is another camellia, *C.* × *williamsii* 'St Ewe', but the harmony is not obvious here, as its leaves are matt and its phlox-pink trumpets single. It continues the camellia theme but its floral style is echoed in that of the dwarf rhododendrons at its feet, whose flowers are also pink, single and trumpet-shaped.

The garden is now beginning to take on a distinct character and is reflecting the tastes of the gardener.

As happens with so many of us, the owner has inherited a dominant plant that it would have been a crying shame to have removed. In this case it is a large specimen of *Rhododendron* 'Lord Roberts', one of the old Hardy Hybrids with dense trusses of funnel-trumpet-shaped flowers in vivid crimson. No matter how major a feature it may be, however, it has been possible for the designer firmly to consider present concerns first (the ferny-gold theme)

Everything goes with everything else and there is nothing that stands out like a sore thumb. Look at the garden from any angle and the plants fit together harmoniously

and then to work back to the rhododendron using the principles of related planting. The two bushes of *Rhododendron* 'Humming Bird', larger than 'Bow Bells' across the lawn, but of almost the same parentage, flower style and colour, link a rhododendron theme at a right-angled axis to the ferny-gold one.

At this stage everything goes with everything else and there is nothing that stands out like a sore thumb. Look at the garden from any angle and the plants fit together harmoniously because each is reinforcing the message generated by others.

Variations on a Theme
There are many ways in which the planting can be developed from here. One is to pick up the acid soil-ericaceous theme set by the camellias and rhododendrons and develop it a little further by the addition of *Pieris* 'Bert Chandler' to the south of the 'Lord Roberts' rhododendron. The flamboyant, satin-pink spring foliage of this pieris needs a green background and, at this point, it has become necessary from a practical point of view to provide some trees to shade the southern end of the garden. A 'woodsy' feel to the whole planting has already been established, so the introduction of a tree at this point, not related in physical terms to anything else, but fitting in with the whole intangible sense of the garden, will maintain the harmony.

Betula utilis jacquemontii, a birch with a beautiful, pure white trunk, will start to protect the woodland plantings and will provide the green background against which the daring foliage of the pieris can be displayed. That is not all. The pink pieris leaves have a white phase between the pink and their subsequent green. Not only will this birch enhance the pinkness of the pieris, it will also relate directly to its whiteness, if only for a short time.

In the corner is *Acer griseum* and, next to it, another birch, *Betula albo-sinensis*. These two trees, neither of which is large, but both of which provide some shade, carry on the motif of beautiful bark. Each has bark that peels in papery curls; the acer's is deep, shining mahogany, curling to orange-mahogany, while that of the birch is orange-pink, curling to bright orange. They are superb when leafless in winter, but especially so when the sun strikes through their curled flakes of bark, turning them into myriad tiny banners of fire.

A path wanders here, so that these effects can be relished. Across it, next to the pieris, is another acer, this time *Acer palmatum* 'Senkaki'. This carries on the bark theme, but in a different way, as every twig and branch is bright, coral red. Opposite, across the path again, is *A. negundo* 'Flamingo', a tree whose foliage is delightfully variegated in cream and soft pink, recalling for several months the colours of the pieris, not least when that shrub, loaded with flower buds, waits patiently all winter for its brilliant turn to come.

Across the lawn is *Acer palmatum* 'Atropurpureum', picking up the emphasis on acers, but

introducing purple foliage. This will be the only 'mention' of this foliage colour. It is not easy to manage and is all too easily overdone with just one brushstroke too many. Here it stands alone but is linked, particularly in autumn, when its palmate

Related planting works wherever you can make a garden. You would not use exactly the same plants in Greenwich, Connecticut as you would in Greenwich, London, England, but you can apply the same principles

leaves, now turned to fiery red, answer the canary gold message from the similarly shaped foliage of 'Senkaki'.

Beyond the feet of the golden robinia, early summer sees a generous planting of the candelabra primula, *Primula bulleyana*. Its yellow flowers, set in concentric whorls on two-foot stems, will be followed by yellow day-lilies of the less blowsy kind, and this planting spreads round the corner of the lawn, linking the narrow border with its broad counterpart. This motif glides into hostas, whose variegated leaves extend the excursion into variegation already encountered then allows for the introduction of meconopsis, purely on the grounds that everyone knows how well primulas and meconopsis go together, whether in the wild or in cultivation.

The blue foliage of *Chamaecyparis lawsoniana* 'Pembury Blue', next to our juniper 'Old Gold', the original central link in the thread of gold, is enhanced in late summer when the lacecap hydrangea 'Blue Wave' decks itself in lacy wreaths of misty blue. Lacecaps have a woodland air about them that is lacking in the mophead hydrangeas and they are perfect neighbours for the hart's tonge ferns. Still, mopheads have a definite place in the garden, and the owner of this one happens to adore 'Madame E. Mouillière', whose heads of white change to the subtlest lime green as winter approaches and last in that state for weeks.

After all, if you cannot do as you wish in your own garden and feel bound by convention, no matter how advanced that convention may be,

The peeling bark of *Acer griseum*

Primula bulleyana **in a related planting where foliage and flowers provide a rich interplay**

what is the point of it all? Our rebel plants the white hydrangea and devil take the hindmost. The individual note, the signature, is what lifts a garden above all artifice and infuses it with art.

Meanwhile, the burgundy-tipped, grey foliage, small, dark-pink flowers and massed red hips of *Rosa glauca* (which used to be *R. rubrifolia*) echo all sorts of hints from the further parts of the garden – the variegations of the pieris and *Acer negundo* 'Flamingo', the blue-grey of 'Pembury Blue' and the bloom on the leaves of the smaller rhododendrons. It provides shade for *Primula pulverulenta*, a rose-pink candelabra primula that nods acquaintance to the distant yellow primulas, thus reinforcing the link between the two golden trees.

Opposite and next to the house, where their wonderful perfumes can be best enjoyed, are some Gallica roses, old fashioned in their lavender pink and deep parma violet, heralded, oh so gently, by *Rosa glauca* and there just because they are beautiful.

Matters of Principle

This is a garden in a certain style, but it does not matter what your preference is, the principle is the same. It would have been perfectly possible for the juniper to have been the jumping-off point for the development of a mediterranean-style garden, all hot and gravelly and full of strong verticals, aromatic, grey foliage and patches of hot colour

panting in the sun. 'Lord Roberts' would have had to have gone, but then we must not feel slavishly bound to the legacies of previous occupiers of our gardens.

To be personal again, I love 'woodsy' gardens on acid, leafy soils. Perhaps this influenced the way I constructed this example. However, I am equally fond of hibiscus, bauhinias, kapok trees and tropical palms growing on sand and crumpled coral. Given the garden flora of Florida or St Lucia, I would apply the same system. The result might veer towards rain forest, or it might twinkle with jewelled lizards among aloes and sea grape; no matter. Related planting works wherever you can make a garden. You would not use exactly the same plants in Greenwich, Connecticut as you would in Greenwich, London, England, but you can apply the same principles.

Related planting allows plants that are strong individuals to play a co-operative part in the garden. If it is planned properly, there should be no rogues, such as a sudden *Crocosmia* 'Lucifer' shouting the scarlet odds all over the place and being unsufferably anti-social. Such hefty accents are integrated by relationship to others. In this case 'Lucifer' would be intriguingly juxtaposed with the sinfully unclerical dahlia, 'Bishop of Llandaff', whose wicked red owes more to Beelzebub than episcopacy. It in turn, linked by its quality of being a dahlia to

Related plantings liberate us from a gardenscape of mauves, pinks, far too much white and tired greys. 'Taste' is the refuge of those who lack competence with colour

the burnt orange of 'Authority', and thence to the soft yellow of 'Vigor', would be related to the cool, peachy yellow of *Crocosmia* 'Solfaterre', whose smoky-bronze leaves relate back again to the Bishop's deep, red-bronze foliage.

Such related plantings liberate us from the mournful passivity of those who insist on a gardenscape of mauves, pinks, far too much white and tired greys. 'Taste' is the refuge of those who lack competence with colour. Strangely enough, you do not hear of Matisse being mentioned in the same breath as 'bad taste', yet the very people who would give their eye teeth for one of his paintings, in which raw, vivid colour is celebrated with complete lack of inhibition, turn their noses up at vivid, unadulterated colours in the garden. Mondrian tried in the most direct way to teach us what you can do with strong tones and seems, at least with the gurus of garden colour, to have failed dismally.

Above all, Gertrude Jekyll, who had more to say about the use of colour in the garden than anyone, is cited today as an apologist for pastel shades. She was anything but that. To read her work is to learn how to relish the crescendo in garden composition, without which there can be no diminuendo. To raise her up as the champion of monotony is tragic.

She would start in the distance with blue and grey, to enhance the feeling of distance, and use softer colours in the further reaches of a border. Towards the centre the tones would gradually strengthen until, as with the soaring arpeggios favoured by the early symphonists that so inspired Mozart, there would be a great paean of vividness, dropping as quickly again to variations on quieter themes.

Of course, we must not expect too much of ourselves. We are, most of us, some distance short of the talent that Miss Jekyll deployed with such personal modesty. Nevertheless, gardening should be fun, and a way of finding joyful expression in the colours, shapes and textures of plants is to be welcomed, not spurned as 'suburban'.

By thinking about relating plants one to another according to their colours, foliage and form we can enjoy brightness as well as restraint and are unlikely, in achieving harmony and balance, to overdo things. Such inbuilt safety measures also preserve the impact of the individual plant, rather than diminish it.

ABOLISHING PLANT PIGEONHOLES

Whether we like it or not, it is difficult to discuss plants without classifying them as shrubs, perennials, bulbs and so on. Indeed, the organisation of this book recognises such categories and unashamedly uses them. Both for the author and for you who read it, the pigeonholes into which we put plants make for easier reference.

We are the better gardeners, though, if we are capable of the mental gymnastics that allow us to

make use of the division of plants into different kinds for the purposes of study, ordering catalogues and finding our way round the garden centre, while at the same time forgetting them when it comes to planning and planting.

'Treat it like a plant' is the sort of advice that allows you to set large-flowered clematis to scrambling through trees and cut lettuce from among the fuchsias

When I was in my gardening infancy, the great Scottish nurseryman, Alex Duguid, presented me with a plant of *Campanula zoysii*, a rare and exquisitely beautiful campanula from high in the Julian Alps on the borders of Austria and Slovenia. It is one of the minor holy grails of alpine gardening and thought of as tricky and temperamental.

I was humble in my thanks and tentative in my request for guidance. To my question, 'How should I grow it?' Alex replied in his quiet, Deeside brogue, 'Treat it like a plant'.

The campanula lived for several years, happily ensconced in a sunny raised bed in a compost that consisted of fifty percent tufa dust and with its roots under a tufa rock. Had I followed the conventional wisdom, it might well have languished in a pot in the alpine house, misunderstood, homesick, and drawn up out of character. As it was, its curious, pinch-mouthed, crystal-blue bells sat snugly close to the white tufa, rubbing aristocratic shoulders with *Potentilla nitida rubra* from the Dolomites.

Certainly it had been allowed to fall into the 'alpines' category; its demise would have been precipitate if it had not. On the other hand it was not assigned a pigeonhole labelled 'tricky rarities for the alpine house', and for that reason lived long before being lifted, divided and replanted. 'Treat it like a plant' may sound trite, even arch, but it is not. It is sound advice.

It is the sort of advice that allows you to look out for herbaceous clematis, grow dahlias among the

A truly mixed border: annuals, perennials, shrubs, clipped hedges – even trees – in a range of shapes and colours, blending harmoniously together

'perennials', set large-flowered clematis to scrambling through trees, thread bulbs among shrubs and promptly forget them, grow crab apples as espaliers along the path, use 'Coral Prince' kale and 'Osaka Red' cabbage as bedding plants, and cut lettuce from among the fuchsias.

Freedom of Choice

Just as related planting frees you from prejudice against strong, clean colour, so decategorising plants lets you express yourself in new, exciting ways. To a large extent the movement away from segregation is under way in gardening, perhaps mirroring the kind of change that is sweeping through human relations throughout the world. The advent of the mixed border has injected much needed life into the rather tired idea of the shrubbery; bright herbaceous plants now take over in mid-summer where before everything went dark. Even more tellingly, shrubs, trees and bulbs have invaded the hallowed ground of the herbaceous border. It is the same phenomenon from another

[The gardener] may become more and more seized of the sheer fun that can be had from splashes of colour for its own sake, that can be changed around entirely from year to year as the whim strikes

angle, but implies not merely a lengthening of the season beyond four or five months but also a way in which we can aim for the year-round garden, with the year seen as a circle and not as a line with a beginning and end.

In planning, especially when working out a scheme of related planting, thinking of plants as plants and not as annuals, shrubs and so on frees the mind from a whole series of obstacles to free-ranging thinking. Annuals provide a good example of how such an obstacle can exist unrecognised.

As mixed borders proliferate – and one is heartily grateful for them and to those who, like Christoper Lloyd, pioneered and popularised them – bulbs, trees and perennials rub shoulders with shrubs and shrub roses. Perennial plants of annual duration in the open garden – dahlias, osteospermums and gladioli among others – are given their rightful

place, and experiment is the order of the day, with the boundaries of hardiness being pushed back with each year that passes. Where, though, are the annuals?

It is just not possible to manage a mixed border properly without creating gaps. A purely herbaceous border of the old sort need have no discontinuities, as the plants, split into divisions every three years or so, occupy allocated areas of ground that can be precisely defined. Few will exceed their territories by much if anything before they are, once again, rousted out of bed like old soldiers, drilled into ranks and sent back to the parade ground.

A mixed border must have gaps because the shrub element consists of individuals that start small and grow steadily. Unless you are forever lifting and moving shrubs – a job that becomes less enticing as both you and they get older – allowance must be made for them to expand. Bulbs and perennials will do the job of filling in, of course, but it is not a good idea to dig and delve close to the root systems of shrubs.

It is much better to sow hardy annuals in shallow drills where you want them to grow for the summer. You can make exactly the right allowance for space, the soil in the root area of the shrubs will not be disturbed, even when you pull the plants up in autumn, and a whole new dimension is added to the border.

Of course, the plantsman will be hard to persuade of the merits of this idea and it would be foolish to try. However, during his growth in gardening to encompass the better aspects of the designer, he may become more and more seized of the sheer fun that can be had from splashes of colour for its own sake that can be changed around entirely from year to year as the whim strikes.

Annuals qualify as plants just as well as shrubs, trees, and the rest. They are not, in general, of the sort about whose foliage you would rave, but some are. *Ricinus communis*, the castor oil plant, has large, palmate leaves with a distinct air of the tropics. The variety 'Carmencita' has beautifully bronzed foliage and is as handsome as many a plantsman's darling. It is a half-hardy annual whose planting will cause a little disturbance, but it can be well away from where damage might occur, surrounded by hardy annuals that can spread into the domain of the nearby shrubs.

Such superb plants get a bad name when used by the sort of parks authority whose colour sense is about equivalent to that of a cave bat. Putting 'Carmencita' in the centre of a round, isolated bed whose only other occupants were African marigolds of an orange seen elsewhere only in chemical effluent was not a good idea. Carrying out the same theme on every traffic circle in the administrative area was an environmental disaster. We advocate the thinking use of strong colours, but there is a limit.

Perhaps there is a prejudice against annuals simply because of the perpetrations of public planting. Certainly those who are capable of using 'suburban' as a pejorative term are likely to be extremely sensitive to being thought of as remotely on the same planet as municipal parks departments. And yet they should make a point of visiting the towns and cities where great plantsmen and gardeners have learned their jobs, such as Brighton, England, or Edinburgh, Scotland, and too many North American cities to mention. There they will find annuals deployed with finesse, fully integrated and treated like plants.

GARDEN FEATURES AND STRUCTURES

————— ❧ —————

Any sensible person has to admit from the outset that a home garden is not just a place for plants. It is, at best, part of a unit with the house; at worst a playground with a repair shop and forecourt. A garden, unless it stands alone as a horticultural institution of some sort, is always the result of compromise.

Nevertheless, setting aside the minimalist schools of gardening, in which plants are largely an intrusion, the garden is the place where we grow and display plants for our own pleasure and that of those who visit us or just pass by. The most enlightened efforts to display them to the best advantage and maximise the effect that each has on those who see it will be spoiled if the setting is mundane, untidy, or sloppily laid out.

Good gardening is often boring, and the chores that have to be done if a garden is to be effective in its impact are the most boring of all. If there is a lawn it absolutely must be kept neatly mown and its edges cleanly trimmed. Anything less is like exquisite tailoring on a man badly in need of a hair-

A short pergola emphasising a feature or a group of plants. It will have even more force if it is repeated beyond the subject

cut: seedy, phoney and just a little grubby. Hedges must be trim, paths weedless, but above all the lines of the design must not become obliterated.

————— ❧ —————

Structures and features that are not integrated into a harmonious whole in the garden will greatly detract from the effectiveness of the plantings, no matter how well thought out they may be

————— ❧ —————

All that is fairly fundamental and few keen gardeners fall down on maintenance unless they have no choice through illness or other misfortunes. What is not so readily realised is that structures and features that are not integrated into a harmonious whole in the garden will greatly detract from the effectiveness of the plantings, no matter how well thought out they may be.

One of the most common faults is the pergola that leads nowhere. A pergola is a major feature that really should have a raison d'être. It should lead, if not to somewhere, then at least from it. What that means is that a pergola can lead from the house to the swimming pool or from the swimming pool to the garden as a whole. If you think a swimming pool is too grand a concept, substitute your own imagery.

It can, as at the gardens of the Royal National Rose Society near St Albans, England, lead from the garden as a whole to an ornamental pond, round it, and on again into the garden. The whole idea of the structure is that it is a partially covered walk; it is there because it is a thoroughfare. A pergola that is put up for the sake of having a pergola seldom gets walked under, as to do so is an artificial activity. 'When you've finished your drink, mother-in-law, we can go to the pergola and walk under it.' One feels it must have been just such an inconsequential alley that prompted Gertrude Jekyll's famous reply when asked her opinion of pergolas, 'They drip'.

The nowhere-pergola sticks up from the garden like an abandoned tram. Similarly, the rock-bun rock garden has a scrapyard look about it. Suddenly there is this heap of soil with rocks stuck in it like

Integrating an alpine bed into lawns and general borders using the principles of 'related planting'

1	*Hypericum olympicum*	3a	*Narcissus* 'Mount Hood'
1a	*Hypericum* 'Hidcote'	4	*Campanula cochleariifolia*
2	Alpine dianthus	4a	*Campanula persicifolia*
2a	Border pinks	5	*Euphorbia myrsinites*
3	*Narcissus* 'April Tears'	5a	*Euphorbia wulfenii*

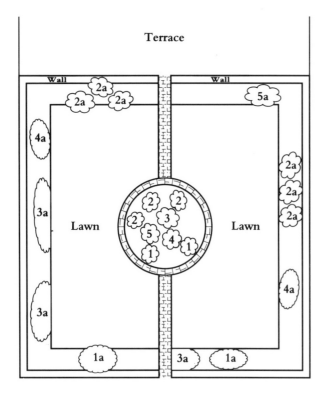

currents. The plants bear no relationship to any others in the garden and are often untended, sad and suffering from second-degree burns. Alpine and rock plants can easily be made to relate to other plants, even at a distance.

For example, *Hypericum olympicum*, only 30cm (1ft) tall, but with large, bright yellow flowers in summer, will relate readily to *Hypericum* 'Hidcote', a shrub usually of 120cm (4ft) in height, with

If you want to make a rock garden, see to it that it looks as though the rocks protruded naturally from the surrounding earth thousands of years before the house was even thought of

golden yellow saucers all summer, even though its rocky site is some distance away from the border in which its larger cousin grows. As long as one glance can take both in at the same time, the association – the link – works.

The best endeavours will fail, however, if the rock-bun is ludicrously out of context, as it so often is. This is no treatise on rock-garden making and it is not even entirely a question of making one; a formal, flat, round scree with radiating paths can be perfectly in tune with, say, a small, square, low-walled garden with borders all round.

Such a garden is illustrated here. The only plants shown are those alpines and border plants that form mutual links. All that is necessary is to use enough of these to integrate the features of the garden; everything else can conform to whatever plan the gardener has in mind for the central scree and the surrounding borders. In this example, although the planting is an invention, the layout is strongly based on part of Geoff Hamilton's famous television garden at Barnsdale, England. Although he often has to erect unrelated structures for professional reasons, his flair for creating harmonious planting is nowhere more marked than close to his house.

If you want to make a rock garden, see to it that it looks as though the rocks protruded naturally from the surrounding earth thousands of years before the house was even thought of. A rock garden should

look as though the only thing you could do with the outcrop was to make it into a home for alpines. It should never appear the result of having felt that a rock garden was a *sine qua non*.

The 'Modern Citizen' part of our brain provides us with an editing facility that makes it bearable for us to live in the modern world. We can live surrounded by rectilinear fences, faced with flat walls, or with our deep desire for green satisfied by a square trimmed to a more even finish than could be managed by the most meticulous sheep. In order to survive we have to make such adjustments. Notwithstanding all that, outrageous anomalies are offensive.

The garden is a 'Modern Citizen' framework in which the 'Old Adam' mind attempts to operate, and in general does pretty well. One accommodation it reaches with its civilised counterpart occurs when it acquiesces in accepting the inevitable appurtenances of latter-day living, while tending to reject intrusive artifacts. In other words, it tells you not to worry about the fence but to get rid of those damn gnomes.

THE VALUE OF PLANNING

Gardens that just grow – as Topsy would have had it – usually look like it. Sometimes the result is astonishingly good, but it is a rare occurrence when a gardener of great flair lacks foresight. Usually the best gardens, in which the plants are happiest and shown off to the best advantage, were planned.

This does not necessarily mean that hours have been spent with drawing board and instruments. It

Beth Chatto's remarkable garden near Colchester, England, is a superb example of how careful planning can create a scene of careless rapture. The most natural plantings are usually the result of much thought having been given to all the characteristics of each plant and to its potential for relating to the others. To achieve art in gardening it is an advantage to take an artless approach, but it must be planned

certainly does not imply that everything must be in place on paper or in the mind's eye from the very beginning. What it does mean is that the characteristics of the plants – tangible and intangible – should be borne in mind throughout, from the first inklings to the onset of the garden's maturity.

Foresight will result in well-furnished, balanced trees and shrubs that have not grown one-sided from overcrowding or stunted from frequent moving. It will prevent the dreadful situation in which people find themselves when they have hinged their entire plan on a major plant or group of plants, only to find that the benighted things loathe the conditions and dwindle sullenly, finally to succumb to terminal homesickness. It will also prevent the intrusion of irrelevant, misplaced, or plain ugly garden features.

If a garden is to bewitch, inspire, allure and exhilarate, as indeed it should, it will only do so if care has been taken to look into the future and don the cloak of patience. Instant gardens only beguile for an instant and quick results often foretell failure. The garden that would make Mr Mole hold up his paws and exclaim, 'Oh my, Oh my, Oh my!' is one into which has gone much thought, enough research and a great deal of love.

CHAPTER 3

―∾―

TREES
AND
SHRUBS

―∾―

*'A woodland in full color is
awesome as a forest fire, in
magnitude at least; but a single
tree is like a dancing tongue of
flame to warm the heart.'*

HAL BORLAND,
Sundial of the Seasons

Fushia magellanica 'Variegata' and *Berberis thunbergii*
'Silver Beauty' cooperating to display much of what is
best in shrubs: flowers, foliage, fruits, autumn colour
and that indefinable touch of character

In every novel there is a critical point at which the reader is either hooked until the last page or lost for ever. It has much to do with credibility. What happens is that you give the author a fair crack of the whip for a few chapters, but if the plot does not hold water or the characters are poorly drawn, you suddenly lose interest.

This book is no novel, but at this point you may well wonder what on earth is going on. You have come thus far, hand in hand with the author, trusting his assertions that plants work best in harmonious combination, and fully prepared to pitch the separate categories of plants out of the window in favour of a more holistic point of view. Suddenly you are confronted with a chapter heading that seems to lead firmly back to square one.

Well, it doesn't. From now on you are assumed to be a disciple of the harmonious disposition of

---

You are prepared to try your hand at related planting, you feel yourself to be well out of the 'pastels-for-safety' school, and you rejoice. . . in the prospect of gardening for yourself and those close to you rather than for potential critics

---

plants and to be firmly set on the path of looking at the garden as a whole and not as a set of uncoordinated features. You are prepared to try your hand at related planting, you feel yourself to be well out of the 'pastels-for-safety' school, and you rejoice, if you did not already, in the prospect of gardening for yourself and those close to you rather than for potential critics.

You are probably also feeling that it is going to be fun to seek out plants with charisma and to look for what it is that distinguishes the long-term asset from the short-term flower bearer. However, when it comes right down to it you will be looking at individual plants as you choose them and you will have to recognise categories because they are what you find in catalogues and garden centres. Nevertheless, while selecting an individual plant, never lose sight of what you are trying to achieve as a whole.

It is also worth bearing in mind that really close attention to the quality of individual specimens

offered for sale can make a great deal of difference to the final result. *Malus* 'Red Jade', which is a weeping crab apple, will be cheap if it is grafted at 1m (3ft) high, but it will never be any higher unless you train up a new leader – several times. It is much better to pay twice the price and start off with a properly made tree that will have presence and elegance, rather than a poor little travesty that can never be other than an embarrassment.

Our attitude towards plant categories must, to some extent, reflect a divided state of mind. On the one hand we ought never to lose sight of our goal of harmonising all the plants in the garden, whether they be woody, herbaceous, bulbs or annuals; on the other we have to bear in mind that woody plants are permanent elements of the garden framework that become perceptibly larger each year. This factor alone merits their being considered separately.

To compound the apparent heresy, it helps if we distinguish trees from shrubs. This is an almost arbitrary distinction, but one that is, in the end, horticulturally helpful.

A tree is a woody plant with a single, clear stem, whose branches arise well above ground level. A shrub is one with many stems arising at or near the ground. The reason why this is arbitrary in practice is that many shrubs can be made to grow as trees and, equally, many trees will grow as shrubs if they do not receive the correct treatment when young.

An example of just how misleading is this distinction is the disagreement between myself and a most distinguished plantsman-gardener and author, the holder of a very senior and respected position in British horticulture. He maintains that *Magnolia* × *soulangiana* is a shrub; I hold that it is a tree. I know specimens that branch very low down and others that are mighty specimens with single, thick trunks – and so does he. Neither of us is daft enough to say that the other is wrong.

It is, up to a point, an academic difference, although what happens at the propagation stage has a lot to do with it. Gardeners will, however, find significant differences ornamentally. For example, *Betula albo-sinensis*, a birch with beautiful, peeling bark in shades of pink and soft red, has a completely different effect when growing shrubbily with several stems from when it has a single, much stouter trunk. In the former case it has a gentle, intricate appeal; in the latter it becomes an architectural feature.

A pure white form of *Magnolia* x *soulangiana* growing in an English churchyard

Catalogues and books that describe a plant as 'a small tree or large shrub' are not trying to confuse; they are just covering themselves, knowing that either is possible. The difference, strictly speaking, has nothing to do with size; a shrub is not simply a small tree. On the other hand though, it has to be admitted that trees are, on the whole, larger than shrubs.

Catalogues rarely commit themselves to giving a size for a tree or shrub, usually using some vague formula such as 'small, medium or large'. You cannot blame them. After all, it is hard not to be put off when you are told that a tree will grow to 30.5m (100ft). You immediately envisage the occultation of all light through the bedroom window, and pay no attention when the nurseryman adds, 'After a hundred years'. Authors, who hope their works will last slightly longer than annual catalogues, are just as cagey, and in this volume you will find heights of woody plants given according to the formula 'after X years', where X is the number according with the writer's experience or just the one with which he feels safest.

TREES OF CHARACTER

If a garden has trees at all they will be the prime factors in creating its atmosphere. There is a world of difference between a garden furnished with oak and ash and one populated by birches. The former has an altogether heavier, more closed-in feel about it, while the latter is more open and airy. A garden with trees has shady places where plants of the woodland floor can thrive; without them there is a certain monotony.

Of course shrubs create shade, but never convincingly in the absence of trees, and the tendency is for them to give an appearance more like scrub. By their very nature trees have more interesting shapes, and it is these that often create an emphatic impression when a garden is seen for the first time, in a different light, or on one's return from a period of absence.

Tree Shapes

Foliage, flowers, fruits and seasonal colour are all important with trees but, in general, they follow behind shape and habit. Proof of this can be found

There is more than just an aesthetic angle to the choosing of trees with particular shapes. The habits of the trees virtually determine what sort of a garden it is going to turn out to be

in the country person who can recognise deciduous tree species at a distance even during the depth of winter. There will be other clues, such as the thickness and quantity of twiggy growth (as in the comparison between an oak and an ash), but his diagnosis is made in the same way as we know a familiar person at a glance by stance, posture and outline.

Judicious use of tree shapes can make a great deal of difference to the garden scene. They provide variety, architectural interest, mood and varying amounts of shade. They also lend themselves to relationships of form with other trees, with shrubs, and even with the house and its attendant structures.

A tree with a strongly defined shape can do much to enhance and complement the design of a house. It can also emphasise its faults if one is not careful. At its simplest, a strongly upright tree such as a columnar Lawson's cypress or a fastigiate mountain ash will strike just the right note in the garden of a single storey house. As a companion for a narrow, three-storied town house it would look like a caricature.

The same goes for garden features. Flights of steps, falling to link two small terraces, would make a strong pattern of geometrical shapes with straight lines in several planes. Just one weeping tree set within the pattern would introduce curves for contrast and movement to counteract the stillness of the structure. The softness of shoot, leaf and flower would be set against the brick or stone, and a strong vertical accent would deny dominance to the horizontals of the steps and terraces. In such a position only a tree will do; its cleanness of line is essential and a shrub would merely hide the structure and create a muddle.

There is more than just an aesthetic angle to the choosing of trees with particular shapes. The habits of the trees virtually determine what sort of a garden it is going to turn out to be. Admittedly other factors such as density of foliage come into it, but there is no escaping the fact that slim trees permit a different kind of garden from one dominated by trees with spreading branches. Wide-headed trees

The shape and stance of *Aralia elata* cause it to conjure up, at one and the same time, a jungly ambience and a hint of the Orient

will eventually preside over gardens devoted to shade and glade lovers, while narrow ones leave plenty of sunny places for more boisterous plantings. However, assuming that you are going to take a reasonably long-term view and not plant too many trees in the first place, it is fair to say that the effect of a tree's form on us is primarily aesthetic.

Once again, however, it must be said that you cannot derive an idea of how a tree is going to look from seeing a young one in a nursery.

It is difficult enough with our own species. Perhaps a highly experienced granny or a priest with a large parish can tell whether a month-old male child will be a linebacker or a chronic sufferer from kicked sand. Most of us cannot. Still less can we divine, without study or observation, whether a tree will be a hulk or a pole.

It is no good saying, 'Any fool knows what an oak looks like' or, 'Japanese cherries are good small trees'. There are oaks from scrubby bushes to mighty giants, and some Japanese cherries spread widely enough in root and branch for one specimen to take over an entire suburban garden.

When you visit gardens, take a notebook with you and write down the names of trees that appeal to you. You may find one or two difficult to obtain, but in the main it will be a great help towards finding the ones with the right shapes.

You will then see that *Cornus controversa* 'Variegata' is a tree, not a shrub as it is so often described. You will fall head over heels for its horizontal branches, along which emerge branchlets clad in neat,

Cornus controversa 'Variegata' forming the central feature of a foliage tapestry

creamily edged leaves, and you will be prepared to listen when someone tells you that its high price is justified because it is difficult to propagate.

You will reject the blandishments of the sales pitch that shouts the virtues of the blue Atlas cedar, *Cedrus atlantica* f. *glauca*. It may be gorgeously blue; it may look small and cute, but just you wait until it gets its feet under the table and you have to get the contractors in to get rid of it.

But then you will have come to know the upright latticework of *Betula pubescens*, the wide-set branches and flat top of *Acer palmatum*, and the blunt, evergreen arrowhead of *Abies koreana*. You will have found out that nothing grows under the massive blob of dark green that is *Quercus ilex* (the holm oak), and that nothing in the world is going to stop you making a feature of *Prunus serrula*.

Bark, Branches and Light

Prunus serrula is the Tibetan cherry. It does not take over, neither does it cast a dense shade, but makes a round-headed, deciduous tree 15m (50ft) high at the very maximum; it is usually much smaller.

What distinguishes it and attracts unending attention is its bark. It is deep chestnut and has the gloss that you might see on the flanks of a thoroughbred stallion. It peels to reveal this shine, which is that of the new bark, but as often as not it receives a little extra peeling and polishing from human hands, and this is why the most striking specimens are near paths.

Those whose chief delight is flowers tend to dis-

miss its blossoms. They are white and 1.5cm (⅝in) across. This is not large compared with the so-called garden cherries but not bad at all as trees go. Its slender, willow-like leaves are a pleasant change from the dirty washing hung out by *Prunus* 'Kanzan' and others. The leaves cast only a light shade, and that and its neat, round head make it ideal for smaller gardens.

It might be thought of exclusively as a plantman's tree and of little interest to the designer. It is certainly approved of by plantsmen who, as we know, appreciate the finer points of plants. It is, however, ideal as an anchor piece for related planting. Other beautiful barks will pick up its message and so will other cherries of similar persuasion – which is to say those that are closer to nature than the blowsy 'Kanzan'. The colour of the bark can also be relayed in other ways, such as by a nearby bush of *Berberis thunbergii atropurpurea*, whose mahogany-maroon foliage is a touch darker in tone than the cherry's bark but is of the same hue.

Prunus serrula

In fact, *Prunus serrula* is a good illustration of the sort of plant that can bring the plantsman and designer elements of our psyches together. Instead of admiring its excellent characteristics in isolation we begin to look for ways in which it can play a keynote role among other plants, with its own outstanding qualities being celebrated rather than overpowered. Its willowy foliage puts one in mind of *Salix* species, and it is not too big a jump to seek out those with pretty bark, such as *S. irrorata*, a shrub or small tree whose branches are purple, covered subtly with a white bloom. When the leaves have gone, the barks of these two plants will remain, contrasting with one another but reinforcing each other's message.

Prunus serrula has oval fruits, too, and will play its part in autumn, even if it is just to nod a hint towards some more conspicuous crop. Why is it that a tree that is not widely regarded as in the front rank for the garden can give rise to so many ideas? In part the answer is that many trees are highly popular for

The snakebark maple, *Acer pensylvanicum*, in winter. In the form 'Erythrocladum', the young shoots stand out bright crimson against the stems, and the young leaves have a pink tinge. The specific epithet lost its second 'n' when originally named, a mistake which the rules say must be perpetuated

the wrong reasons, such as flamboyance of bloom backed by eleven months of dullness, but it is also because once you start following the strands of re-

Acer palmatum *'Senkaki'* settles down to provide a winter display that is second to none for bewitching tracery, lighting up in the sun to a bright pink lacework

lated planting it is like getting on one of those moving walkways in airports; there is no way off until you get to the end.

Acer griseum is *the* mahogany-barked tree. It has often been blithely recommended in the past when its difficulty of propagation made it hard to come by. Modern methods seem to have overcome the problem (dissecting out the embryo from the seed was a start, in my case increasing germination from 0 to 30 per cent) and it is not only much more easily obtainable, but cheaper.

Its bark must not be given a helping hand in peeling. There is a specimen in the garden at Muckross House, Killarney, Ireland, whose appeal has been almost entirely ruined by the public's stripping the burnt-orange curls from the mahogany trunk and branches. When the sun is behind the tree it is these curly flakes that light it up in a fiery halo. They should be left alone.

This treasure from China, often called the paperbark maple, has no beauty of flower, but that is no bar to its year-round value. In addition to its bark's twelve months of attractiveness, it has charming, trifoliate leaves in dark, almost olive green. These turn, in autumn, to the hotly glowing scarlets and blackish reds of a coal fire at bedtime; a wonderful contrast to the canary yellow of *Acer palmatum* 'Senkaki'.

This latter is either a shrub or a small tree, depending on how it has been 'done' as a youngster. It matters less than with many other woody plants, as it is not the trunk but the branches and branchlets that bear the colour – in this case bright coral-red, from which it gets its name of coral-bark maple. After its buttery autumn show it settles down to provide a winter display that is second to none for bewitching tracery, lighting up in the sun to a bright pink lacework or, when partly clothed in hoarfrost, looking like the work of a prize-winning confectioner.

The maples are a large and diverse group of trees with which few others can compete for all-round performance, even though they are not known for much in the way of flower. They are famous for their autumn colour from the hillsides of Vermont to the arboreta of Europe and the old gardens of Kyoto, and a few are justly renowned for their beautiful bark.

Others however are not so widely appreciated. The snake-bark maples are strangely neglected, even though they are trees with delightfully patterned bark, some of which have brightly coloured leaf stalks, and most of which are superb in autumn. The barks are patterned in thin, interlacing lines of white or russet-red, with backgrounds of green or orange-red. This characteristic, interestingly, is found on both sides of the Pacific, with *Acer grosseri* and *A. g. hersii* being the most frequently grown Chinese species and *A. pensylvanicum* coming from North America. This latter species especially is almost made for modern gardens of limited size, where its jade-green snakeskin bark and bright yellow autumn colour will be major features. It is, however, no lover of chalky soils.

Birches, too, are found all over the northern hemisphere. The lightly branched structures and relatively low ultimate heights of many of them make good garden trees, under which other plants have no difficulty in growing. Among them are some of the most lovely trees of all as far as bark

The maples are famous for their autumn colour from the hillsides of Vermont to the arboreta of Europe and the old gardens of Kyoto, and a few are renowned for their beautiful bark

goes. *Betula pendula*, the European silver birch, is only in the second or third rank, beautiful as it is, for although its bark is silvery white, it is crazed with deep, black fissures.

Other birches have trunks of brilliant, almost pure white. In the garden we designed on p24, *Betula utilis jacquemontii* played a vital part with its

A particularly outstanding form of *Betula jacquemontii*, now properly *B. utilis* var. *jacquemontii*

conspicuous trunk. It is quite one of the most desirable garden trees of all, unmistakable at all times of the year but especially dramatic in winter. Its base makes the most delightful background for little daffodils or dwarf cyclamen and it is an easy matter to integrate it into the rest of your tree planting, especially if its companion is another birch, such as *B. albo-sinensis* or its even more orange form, *B. a-s. septentrionalis*. In larger gardens a group of three or four together makes an unforgettable feature.

There are other birches with white bark, but be sure to do your research before settling on one of them, as they can be quite large. *Betula costata* is magnificent if you have room for it. Its peeling bark is of a rich cream and its autumn colour is warm yellow. The effect of the two together is quite magical, but it will outgrow the 'medium' category eventually. So will *B. ermanii*, the white of whose trunk has a pink tinge. *B. maximowicziana* grows quickly but not too large and has brownish-orange bark. It is the birch with the largest leaves and has the lovely yellow autumn colour that is shared by so many in the genus.

Falling for trees with nice barks is fine, but look out for the pitfalls. You should be able to avoid most of them by exercising your penchant for visualising their eventual neighbours. However, just in case, it is worth reminding ourselves of one or two of them.

Eucalyptus, for example, often have deliciously patterned barks, so much so that Australian foresters classify them as 'iron barks', 'stringy barks' and even 'scribbly barks'. They are highly desirable trees, but they look like no others and can be difficult to fit into the garden. If you get it right they are one of the best arrows in your quiver and you should pay no attention to the 'cognoscenti' who maintain that they have no place in gardens in the northern hemisphere.

One of the best ways of accommodating them is to take their foliage colour as the main focus. This is easy if you plant them against evergreen green backgrounds, as their mostly blue-grey or almost blue foliage will be thrown into dramatic relief. They can then be picked up by the taller blue conifers or have their glaucous grey tones echoed by *Phormium tenax*. As far as bark goes, take the long shoots of *Salix daphnoides*, which are exactly the right purple-violet to match those of the commonly grown *Eucalyptus gunnii*, and you are off and running once again.

Just don't plant a eucalyptus after it is 30cm (1ft) tall. You will either have to cut it back after three years, wait for the forest of new shoots, and select one to start again or, if you have staked it, it will fall down one day when it is just the height you wanted, wrecking everything as it drops. Those same Australian foresters say that the bigger the stake

It is just as mistaken to plant a tree on account of its bark when it is wrong for your garden, as it is to drag a plant screaming into a monochrome border just because it is the right colour

you use on a eucalyptus, the bigger the tree when it falls down. You should also never use manure when planting a eucalyptus, but I won't tell you what they say about that.

It is just as mistaken to plant a tree on account of its bark when it is wrong for your garden as it is to drag a plant screaming into a monochrome

border just because it is the right colour. *Stuartia pseudocamellia* has almost everything – lovely, large, white flowers 5cm (2in) across, wonderful autumn colour, and highly arresting , peeling bark, somewhere between mahogany and terracotta. Unfortunately it cannot be grown in gardens with lime in the soil.

This does not mean that it should not be generally recommended. On the contrary, it is one of the finest small trees you can grow. What it does mean is that your study and research will not be complete until you have found out whether this tree or any other plant you have chosen will tolerate your conditions.

Another major pitfall is to forget the effect of light on trunks and branches. Plant in too dark or dank a place and they will be permanently covered in algae and mosses. Forget the play of sunlight and you will never see the fascinating effects caused by its shining on, through or behind coloured or peeling barks. Plant too densely and you will have to crawl among your trees in order to see the last vestiges of the drama for which you thought you had planned so well. Do not plant too many trees. They grow eventually. Choose a few and take time to select just those that will provide the best year-round value. After all, as Scarlett said, 'Tomorrow is another day'.

CHARACTERFUL TREE FOLIAGE

Generally speaking, the bigger the tree the less impressive are the individual leaves. This is simply because they are further from your eye. However, the leaves become commensurately more important en masse. The impressiveness of large trees is, to quite a major extent, due to the ways in which foliage masses are deployed.

This is not quite the same as overall shape, which is usually the same for a deciduous tree whether it is in leaf or not. With evergreen conifers of the columnar type, foliage distribution can give rise to a layered effect that has nothing to do with the shape or silhouette of the tree. Foliage in large trees is more a matter of texture.

In smaller trees the individual leaves become more important. If the trees are small because of youth the leaves will be conspicuous for a long time but will eventually merge into the texture of the mature canopy. If they are small because that is their nature, their leaves will permanently play a direct part in the foliage relationships at the lower levels of the garden.

It follows that the purchase of larger trees should be looked at from two points of view. In the short term they should be integrated into the surrounding

Larger trees. . . should be integrated into the surrounding plantings; in the long term they will contribute to the upper storey, where the overall character of the garden is so largely determined

plantings of shrubs and perennials; in the long term they will contribute to the character of the upper storey, where the overall character of the garden is so largely determined.

For instance, *Ailanthus altissima*, the tree of heaven, has spectacular foliage when young. A man-high sapling will have pinnate, ash-like leaves 1m (3ft) long and be as exotically jungly a plant as you could imagine. At this stage it is impossible to ignore; its message is far too strong for that. It is no good kidding yourself that it will soon scorch away upwards and let you off the hook. It is fast growing, but not that fast.

When it does reach maturity – and it is a large tree, so be warned – it is all right, but not really that much more dashing than an ash, and nothing like it was when it used to upstage the local shrubs and stuck out like a bronco rider at a hunt ball.

One of the most unusual tree leaves is that of the tulip tree, *Liriodendron tulipifera*. Fundamentally, it has four lobes, but is best thought of as having two small, upward pointing side lobes and one large terminal one that looks as though it has been cut across with an inwardly curving swipe of the knife. The stalks are carried well apart and are long and slender, so there is plenty of flutter and quiver among the large, strangely beautiful leaves.

There is, too, a variegated form, 'Aureomarginatum', whose leaves have soft-yellow margins with just a hint of green. If this tree is grown as a free-standing specimen with no competition at all, the variegation remains effective because the lowest branches will be not very far from eye level. If, on the other hand, it becomes drawn up by adjacent buildings or other trees, the variegation might as well not be there unless you look for it with binoculars.

The lesson is plain. You should choose trees with interesting foliage by all means, but once again plant fewer than you might have thought you could accommodate. The long-term result will be that their foliage will contribute both to the effect of the upper storey of planting – because of the homogeneous appearance of the leaves higher up – and also to the general foliage plan of the garden, because the lower reaches of the tree will be preserved.

Furthermore, be sure that your young tree, so fiercely proud of its precociously developed leaves, is not going to become more conservative in later life. If it is, all is not necessarily lost, as you may be able to garden it into eternal youth.

New Trees from Old

The process is called stooling. All you do is to cut your tree down to ground level or near it every year or two. Just a few trees react to this by producing enormous leaves. It takes a very great deal out of the young tree unless you feed it like a Strasbourg goose, but if you do it will reward you with foliage effects that are second to none.

Essentially the tree must be inherently fast growing, and given to producing over-sized leaves naturally when it is very young. The tree of heaven, *Ailanthus altissima*, will perform well with stooling, as will some of the large-leaved oaks such as the Algerian (*Quercus canariensis*) and the Hungarian (*Q. frainetto*). The classic tree for this treatment, however, is the foxglove tree, *Paulownia tomentosa*.

This is one of the most spectacular hardy trees. The flowers are produced before the leaves; they are just like foxgloves and are borne in large bunches at the ends of the branchlets. The colour is usually described as heliotrope, but is not at all vicious and more of a warm mauve. Unfortunately, the flowers are vulnerable to frost, and as they are formed in autumn and held unopened throughout the winter, they seldom see spring except in mild climates, and even there they often fail.

However, the chief glory of the tree is its leaves. They are large and squarely broad, with three to five very shallow, pointed lobes. They are velvety to the touch and anything from 12cm (5in) wide to twice as much in adult trees.

If you grow it from seed, which is very easy indeed, as long as you treat the seedlings with a fungicide against damping-off, you should let the seedlings grow fast for two or three years, feeding them well. In the early spring of the next year, cut them down to 2.5cm (1in) from the ground. Three or four shoots will arise, of which just one should be selected and the others removed. The shoot will grow to well over 2m (6ft) in a season and carry several enormous leaves 60cm (2ft) across. Hefty manuring should keep them going for years of repeated stooling. A little grove of stooled paulownias is as imposing a mini-jungle as can be devised and is superb between smaller-leaved shrubs or growing near bamboo. Even so, just one specimen is a force to be reckoned with and a lovely background for *Iris sibirica*.

Maintaining the Balance

A balance should be struck between evergreen and deciduous trees. Too great a preponderance of evergreens leads to a heaviness and dullness about the garden, and the seasons are not allowed their sway. If the trees all lose their leaves in winter the place will feel cold, draughty and bare. How successfully the balance is struck depends to a large extent on climate, as deciduous trees are mostly the hardiest, while many evergreens have difficulty coping with freezing winds. Conifers are an exception, as most of them are successfully adapted to preventing the loss of water which is the real killer in freezing conditions.

Conifers, like anything else, are easily overdone. A style of gardening that is now, thank heaven, passé, was the conifers-with-heathers garden, in which cones, columns, domes, platforms and obelisks would thrust upward from heathery patchwork quilts like the elements of some educational game for three-year-olds. The foliage had impact, that's for sure, but just what kind depended on the sensibilities of the observer.

The taller conifers, however, are valuable additions to the garden scene and help to set the evergreen/deciduous balance, while the dwarf conifers can play a leading part in integrating the rock garden into the garden as a whole. No group of garden plants that I know of is without its value, but they can all suffer from being done to death.

Trachycarpus fortunei, **the Chusan palm, is the only palm hardy in the British Isles, with representatives from Cornwall to Northumberland. It will stand cold, but must be sheltered from wind. Its fan-shaped fronds, well over 1m (3ft) across, provide an exotic feature second to none. Flowering is of secondary importance and does not occur in young trees. The tallest in cultivation, over a century old, are about 12m (40ft) high**

Those who garden where there is little frost are often guilty of planting too many evergreen trees. The temptation is understandable, as it is greatly satisfying to see tender subjects growing to maturity when they would be killed outright elsewhere. The result, however, is dull unless leavened in some way. In tropical gardens there is so much more scope for using widely divergent forms, such as the travellers' palm, baobabs and banyans, which are utterly fascinating of themselves as well as in combination. Gardens in more temperate climes, where the range of evergreens is relatively limited, demand a deciduous element if they are not to seem out of place and depressing.

AUTUMN COLOUR IN TREES AND SHRUBS

There is no denying the beauty of autumn leaves in higher latitudes. The greater the difference in temperature between summer and winter and between autumn nights and days, the better the colour will be. The more deciduous trees and shrubs are grown, the more colour there will be.

In the forest, it is trees that create the dazzling displays that so entrance visitors to northern North America. In gardens, the combined effect of trees and shrubs is what gives the fall its full majesty.

However, a word of caution is called for. In the best climates for gardening the temperature gradients are often not ideal for the formation of bright colours. Where it is mild and almost frost-free, birches will glow with gold and many maples will flame redly, but mountain ashes will simply drop their leaflets while still green. The garden that is blessed with a kind climate will not be a good one for autumn colour, and a great deal of the tree and shrub foliage will turn brown.

Furthermore, good gardening climates are often maritime. This not only means that they are likely to be mild, but also that they are erratic. If you live in Britain or Ireland, the north-western part of North America, many areas of New Zealand, or anywhere else where the weather is at the mercy of the ocean's whims, you are highly likely to find that there are many years when autumn leaf colour is disappointing.

None of this is said to put you off. It is, once again, a warning against going overboard for a par-

ticular range of effects. It is all too easy during the autumn planting season to succumb to the perfectly fair blandishments of those who would like to interest you in colourful leaf fall. Gardening writers return to it year after year and nurseries emphasise this highly desirable characteristic on their bed labels and in their catalogues. There is nothing wrong with that. Where you must not go wrong is in failing to appreciate that autumn colour is extremely fleeting at best, and at worst it can be, in any given year, almost completely lacking.

Then again, some trees and shrubs are more reliable in this respect than others. Some, such as the Japanese maples and deciduous azaleas, are as dependable as it is possible to be, while others vary between being stars and broken reeds.

For all these reasons it is not practicable to try to fit autumn colours into your related plantings. It is much better to use them sparingly and to the greatest possible dramatic effect so that, in good years, the fall will be a memorable occasion and by no means routine. Where gardeners plant too lavishly for autumn effects they fall between two stools. On the one hand the danger of planting for any isolated virtue can lead to a garden that is dull for much of the year, and on the other there may be a series of colourless autumns.

The wisdom of always looking for a strong characteristic other than the one you first think of is even more called for when autumn colour is concerned. If you plant *Euonymus alatus*, do so because

The wisdom of always looking for a strong characteristic other than the one you first think of is even more called for when autumn colour is concerned

the position is ideal for a medium-sized, deciduous shrub with interestingly winged branches and masses of bright red, winged fruits. As a secondary consideration, take care that it will do itself justice as a sensation in flame red should it feel like doing so.

In the average-sized garden it is far better to have just one or two really vivid autumn effects than to create a scene of jazzy muddle. The scenes that stay a long time in the memory are of the single Japanese

maple glowing amid the surrounding green, the ruby dazzle of azaleas against the sedate darkness of hollies, and the gold of *Acer pensylvanicum*, like a roman candle among the trees.

If possible, try to plant the the autumn features where the low sunlight will back-light the leaves. It is not always possible to do this and, at the same time, provide the right contrasting background, but if you can, the effect is one of the most memorable you can contrive in the garden. Back-lighting is a neglected art, one to which we should pay much more attention. Leaves, peeling bark and flowers all become so much more fascinating when lit, as it seems, from within.

Backlit autumn foliage of *Acer palmatum* 'Atropurpureum' in the author's garden. Its foliage turns from bronze-purple to flame red

SHRUBS AND FOLIAGE

Whereas the flamboyance of autumn is just a passing, if very welcome phase, tree and shrub foliage is probably the most important element in the majority of gardens.

The foliage of shrubs plays different roles from those played by trees. Tree foliage has one part to play low down and an entirely different one in the canopy.

The garden divides itself into layers, with shrubs for the most part forming the lower one. In it, they interact with the lower branches of the trees. Of course, this is not as simple as it sounds, as it depends on the size of the garden, the size of the trees, the closeness of the planting, and several other variables. Nevertheless, next time you visit a well-established garden in which there are plenty of trees and shrubs, try to see if you tend to have the shrubs and smallest trees within your more constant field of vision, while having consciously to look up to take in everything taller. You will be almost sure to find that you recognise two distinct layers. It is the lower level of the garden and all its components, whether they be technically trees or shrubs, with which we are concerned here.

This is the green world our ancient selves recognise and in which they feel safe and restful. The heart of a garden's impact is here; its arrangement determines much of how we feel about gardening, the world and ourselves.

If this layer of foliage were just an even green it might be restful enough but would hardly be exciting. What makes it so – and we are leaving out flowers for now, as they do come and go, cliché or not – are the variations on green. The odd non-green accent – so-called purple leaves, true yellow, and so on – is indeed stimulating, but should be used in the service of green. It will have far more impact than if used merely to make an isolated statement about purple or yellow.

The Green Palette

Green varies from almost yellow to near black. There are whole symphonies of colour that can be composed using such a scale. In smaller gardens, if not grander works, compositions in all sorts of moods are still possible, using fewer players. Green can be glossy and rich, as in the trifoliate leaves of *Choisya ternata*, mirror-shiny, as in camellias, polished and olive-toned (*Fatsia japonica*), and silkily smooth, as are many magnolias. It can be like fine velvet (*Hydrangea sargentiana*), silver plated (*Cystisus battandieri*), darkly brooding, as in some hollies, and just plain mid-green.

Texture and colour can be matched, contrasted, compared and reinforced. A holly next to a golden conifer and camellias dazzling whitely in the summer sun, are all highlighted in their stillness by the gentle weave and sway of a weeping birch. Movement is part of the variations on green and so is sound. A papery rustle in bamboo is more urgent and compelling than a whisper among the soft leaves of a maple, even though both are caused by the same gentle breeze.

The message sent out by uniform greenery contains words like 'ordinary', 'unexciting' and perhaps even 'boring'. Interacting, lively, mobile greens tell of optimism, charm, allure, exhilaration and enchantment.

It is difficult to make mistakes with green. The different greens do not clash. It is perfectly possible for trees and shrubs with leaves that are almost blue to stand in contrast with near-yellow foliage. The brighter the accent that is used to contrast with dark green the better, if liveliness is looked for. However, you can be as subtle as you like, too, using small changes in green to create *chiaroscuro*, (an effect of light and shade), and relying on other things – bark, flowers, fruits and shapes – to strut their stuff against a background of restraint.

So infinite are the ways in which the green heart of the garden can be made to reflect the way you look at the world that to be specific would be merely to offer restrictions to your imagination. Suffice it to say that as long as you bear it in mind and bring to the front of your desiderata, when choosing plants, such things as texture and tone, your garden's message will never be in the 'boring' category.

Coloured Foliage

It is simply because shades of green make up such a delightful palette that foliage of other colours and variegated leaves can, all too easily, be destructive intrusions.

Planting too many yellow-leaved plants destroys the restfulness of the garden and creates a harsh dazzle in which there is the illusion of no shade. There is a cheap, temporary look about the place. Yellow is a bad background against which to enjoy, and sometimes even to see flowers. White and yellow will tend to disappear, red will fade or look tawdry, and you will be left trying to make as much of blue and purple as you can.

'Purple' foliage, which is red mixed with black, brown or blue-green, and not the same purple as you find in flowers, is dangerous in quite the opposite way if overdone. It becomes heavy and oppressive and quickly wipes out any subtleties you may have employed in deploying shades of green. It is an undiplomatic colour with no social graces at all when mob-handed. Individually, however, it may be quietly effective in the right company.

Purple leaves make a much better background for flowers. Reds and pinks are enhanced, whites are

vividly emphasised, and yellows glow triumphantly. Blues are robbed and mauves disappear, but that need not be a problem when purple foliage is used with circumspection.

I cannot abide **Berberis 'Rose Glow'** *and its redolence of the washing-up that follows a children's tea party, but must bow before its staggering sales figures*

One strong purple accent, whether a tree or a shrub, can add immeasurably to the character of a garden, as long as it is never, never put within screaming distance of one with yellow leaves. Plant yellow daffodils at its feet by all means, but do not allow yourself to believe that yellow and purple leaves belong together. They are as compatible as Cain and Abel.

Variegated plants have, for many gardeners, the same sort of attraction that leads other people to collect pot lids or chinoiserie. Unfortunately, as in those fields, the quality is variable, the choice wide, and the prices low. The result is that not just some gardens, but the majority, are overdone with variegation, while a few are sad repositories of the freakish and diseased.

Trees and shrubs with variegated foliage should be planted with specific ends in mind, not because they look intriguing in the garden centre or just 'different'. The leaves can serve to enhance the flowers, as in *Weigela florida* 'Variegata', whose pink, foxglove blossoms are more jewel-like against its grey-green, cream-edged foliage, or can brighten up a dark corner in an interesting way. They can project various messages about the scheme of green of which they are a part, as long as restraint is used. A cacophanous babel is all too often what happens in practice, the result of a failure to realise that distinction is a product of scarcity.

The choice of variegated trees and shrubs is largely a matter of personal taste. There is perhaps no other group of plants among which such strong opinions are expressed. I, for example, positively loathe *Prunus laurocerasus* 'Marble White', yet in all else about plants I defer to the well-known plantsman who named it and who loves it dearly. I cannot abide *Berberis* 'Rose Glow' and its redolence of the washing-up that follows a children's tea-party, but must bow before its staggering sales figures. Still less can I guide you in your choice, but must restrict myself to reiterating resolutely that with variegation, moderation is everything.

Contrast in Form

With shrubs, foliage is closely related to form. Because they branch low down, they are usually furnished with leaves almost to ground level. Even deciduous shrubs tend to be very solid objects, and for the most part there is not a great deal of movement among them. In general, trees move with the wind, shrubs resist it.

Density of foliage is a theme upon which many variations can be composed. The less dense it is, the less it is related to form. An example of this is the contrast between the open-work foliage of a shrubby willow and the opaque mass of a holly. There is plenty of sky or background when you look at a willow; none at all with a holly. The willow becomes partly edited-out as far as structure goes, leaving the holly as the strong feature. Densely foliaged shrubs should be planted as the main structural elements, with those that are less dense being thought of as occupiers of interstitial space.

This is emphatically not to deny how vital it is to choose the less dense shrubs well. The more airy shrubs provide the essential balance for their more dense brethren and, because the majority are deciduous, they are the ones in which the seasonal pageant is most likely to parade. In a way, the strongest elements in garden design form the background for the less strong. They are the constant factors, playing the parts tuxedos do when, as accompaniments to evening gowns, they, by contrasting, display them to the best advantage.

The foliage of shrubs, as well as that of trees, should be watched for density when other plants are to be grown among them. Too many densely foliaged shrubs will create shady spaces between them. There needs to be a leavening of more airy ones so that dappled light reaches the soil, and primulas, snowdrops, Pacific Coast irises, hostas, crocosmias, and the whole host of plants that like just such situations, will not be shaded out, and fail.

The smaller the garden, the fewer shrubs there should be with dense foliage. In a small garden you want to enjoy yourself and grow as many different plants as you can, or at least to keep your options open. Furthermore, it does not take much imagining to realise that dense foliage makes for darkness and heaviness, the very things most to be avoided in small spaces. The reason a lot of us dislike aucubas, which are very fine plants indeed, is because we saw so many of them in small, city front gardens when we were children, grimy with soot, squashed by leaning bicycles, brown of lower leaf from the appreciations of dogs; louring, shivering captives, perversely consumed with envy for the aspidistras trapped indoors.

Leafy Features

Leaf size is not the same thing at all. Dense foliage is dense whether the leaves are large or small. Large leaves do not necessarily constitute dense foliage. *Hydrangea quercifolia*, a ravishing 'lacecap', has leaves like those of an American oak. It still manages to be light of touch, even more so when brushed by a breeze. Immobility is the enemy of lightness in shrubs (although it is a virtue in strongly architectural plants of whatever kind), and denies the play of light and shade that leavens the effect of large but mobile leaves.

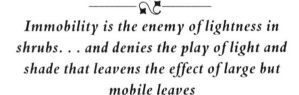

Immobility is the enemy of lightness in shrubs. . . and denies the play of light and shade that leavens the effect of large but mobile leaves

Leaf shape, at the shrub and lower tree level, is something with which one can have the greatest fun. Setting off the oaky, sinuate leaves of *Hydrangea quercifolia* against the still, small, rounded ones of a hybrid of *Rhododendron williamsianum* may seem a good idea, but how about ringing the changes on a hydrangea theme and contrasting them with smoothly lanceolate 'Blue Wave'? Or, possibly, they could proclaim their unbotanical relationship to a stooled Hungarian oak? Or maybe . . .

And so it goes on. Leaves of woody plants vary from the enormous (*Fatsia japonica*) to the minute (several brooms). They can be wavy-edged or perfectly round, long and thin or broad as a spade,

spiny or smooth, heart-shaped, sharply pointed, long, short, rigid or limp. If you are looking for texture, here it is. Play your tunes on these and the shades of green, throw in the occasional coloured note, and you will never ever have to resort to the mediocre. Every one of your shrubs will assert its formidable character and you will have so arranged them that harmony reigns. Meanwhile you had quite forgotten flowers, hadn't you?

WOODY PLANTS AND THEIR FLOWERS

If you were to ask most gardeners what the main attribute of flowers was, they would be fairly certain to answer 'colour'. Indeed, to many gardeners colour is what gardening is all about. Many years of looking after a large garden that was visited by many tens of thousands of people a year led to a private compilation of oft-repeated statements that

The diamond-bright, spring light of south-western Ireland allows the azalea Rhododendron amoenum *to carry off its flamboyant display with aplomb . . .*

back up this observation.

'I like to see a riot of colour', was amazingly frequent. 'It's all about colour, isn't it?' was another, and so was, 'A garden without colour is no garden at all'. Thank heaven for the diverse opinions of mankind! Life would be very dull if there was nobody with whom to disagree. It was just a little hard, however, to refrain from a sharp riposte one blossomy day when the magnolias were magnificently in bloom, many camellias were still flowering, and the scent from the white blossoms of osmanthus wafted widely on the spring air. 'Excuse me', said a young man, with that ominous politeness only the English can manage, 'I've done the walk through the woods; perhaps now you would tell me where the garden is'.

Density and Style

Colour in trees and shrubs is not, except in certain cases, the most important aspect of flowering. That distinction belongs to density of flower. The more any given portion of the surface area of a shrub is covered in flowers, the more will be its impact *in terms of colour*. The more densely packed the flowers are, the more the exact hue, tone or tint will matter. To a certain extent, their individual size will be less effective and their style – the way each flower is made – will be of minor consequence.

Equally, the more the flowers or individual clusters are separated and spread out, the less their colour matters, but the size and style of the flower or cluster become much more important. In trees and shrubs whose flowers are solitary, size and style are paramount; colour, while still important, becomes secondary.

The most extreme examples of density of flowering are the Japanese azaleas, particularly those known as the Kurume azaleas, and especially a group of them called the Wilson Fifty, after E. H. Wilson, the celebrated plant hunter, who introduced them from Japanese gardens in 1920. Many of them – such as *Rhododendron* 'Kirin', a 'hose-in-hose' (one flower inside another) double in shell pink (Wilson 22), 'Kure-no-Yuki', similar, but white (Wilson 2), and 'Ho-o' (also known, under-

. . . while in the softer, dreamier sunshine of an English garden, blue hydrangeas reflect the summer sky . . .

. . . and *Kalmia latifolia*, shadily sheltered, is more modestly showy, but still a shrub of great floral beauty

The exception that proves the rule. The effectiveness of *Garrya elliptica*, which flowers in winter, derives from its covering itself with tassel-like inflorescences. It is the shape and number of the flower clusters, not their colour, that give the shrub its dramatic impact, chiefly because, in winter, any flowers at all are highly significant. The shape and size of each individual flower, however, is of no consequence

The flowers of *Fremontodendron* 'Pacific Sunset' would be arresting no matter what colour they were. Each one has its own impact, which is primarily due to size and shape. The impact of *Solanum crispum* 'Glasnevin', on the other hand, depends on the flowers being gathered into clusters. In its case it is the colour of the individual flower, more than its size or shape, that determines the plant's floral effect

standably, as 'Apple Blossom'), pink with a white throat (Wilson 9) – are shrubs of less than 1m (3ft) that become entirely covered with blossom in mid-spring. The effect of a group of them is utterly ravishing. What you see is billows of pure colour with no green at all. As far as their dramatic effect goes, it matters not one whit what shape, size or style the flowers have; their colour is everything.

Among the Hardy Hybrid rhododendrons (Hardy Hybrid is a proper name, not a description), the density of flower is still very high, but green lacunae appear because flowering does not take place all over the shrub, but in clusters on some of the branches. How dense the flowering will be depends, to a large extent, on the size of the clusters (trusses). These plants are the product of many crosses and experiments, mostly carried out before 1940, in which hardiness was sought along with the reliable production of very large trusses.

Each truss looks rather like one of those frilled

The simple, loose trusses of a species rhododendron or simple hybrid have a greater appeal to many eyes than the very large, round, packed flower heads of the Hardy Hybrids, which seem to owe little of their artificial appearance to nature

rubber bathing caps that ladies wore in the 1950s. If you were not there to see them, never mind, you can trust the simile. En masse, they turn the rhododendron into a beacon of almost solid colour. However, because it is not quite solid, the style of the individual clusters becomes apparent and many people, including some whose opinions carry much weight, dislike them. Even though they may ad-

mire the colour, they will dismiss such a plant as vulgar, garish and overdone.

Given the identical colour, they will feel much happier with a less highly bred rhododendron with looser trusses in which the individual flowers are more readily discernible, and fewer in number. They prefer this style of flowering. They will probably greatly admire the Loderi hybrids, in which the individual blooms are very large indeed, and which are supremely elegant, aristocratic shrubs that would not be seen dead in bathing caps.

The Plantsman's Choice

The more a shrub's flowers remain simple and capable of being appreciated individually, the more it will appeal to the plantsman. He will not care too much what colour the flower is, as long as it is not violent puce or vicious magenta. Of course, a good, firm colour will win his heart, but it must be combined with intangible qualities such as elegance and poise. The size of the shrub must be in proportion to the foliage and it will be judged for the ratio

Ceanothus arboreus 'Trewithen Blue' is a shrub whose floral impact is exclusively derived from the large clusters into which its flowers gather. Each bloom is only 3mm (1/8in) across

between flower size and the overall density of flowering. The plantsman is the last person to reject one of the Wilson Fifty for having too many flowers, but he may prefer, as a shrub on the same scale, a rhododendron like 'Humming Bird', which has elegant, dangling, rounded, individual bells. He will not be the least interested in a Hardy Hybrid.

Perhaps the ultimate in the appeal of size and style of flower is among the magnolias. There are few spectacles more breathtaking than a fully grown tree magnolia in spring. The domed cloud of white, pink or a mixture of white and purple provides a scene of sumptuous, compelling beauty. Each bloom, wonderful in its simplicity, majestic in size, and often as strangely tropical as the much more complicated flower of an orchid, is an individual delight. The impact of the mass of colour is tremendous, but we still seek the single, mysterious bloom.

With summer-flowering magnolias there is none of the same panache. The flowers of *Magnolia sinensis* and *M. wilsonii* dangle like paper lanterns, each one a miracle of floral perfection. There is no chromatic fanfare with them, no riotous greeting of spring. They quietly, almost demurely celebrate the gentle air of summer and invite you to share it with them. The evergreen, yellow-flowered magnolias, *M. grandiflora* and the rarer *M. delavayi*, are

Camellia japonica 'Lady Hume's Blush', also known as 'Incarnata', is the result of centuries of camellia breeding in China, whence it was brought to the West in 1806. It is an example of the best of the style called Formal Double. In shade it lacks the impact of plants in sunny positions, which become densely covered in the demurely coloured blooms

Magnolia grandiflora *and the rarer* M. delavayi. . . *are among the most ravishing of all trees and shrubs because the form and overwhelming size of their flowers are irresistible. Grandeur is far more seductive than mere colour*

still more reticent. They are not given to overt display, but bear their flowers a few at a time over a long period. And yet they are among the most ravishing of all trees and shrubs because the form and overwhelming size of their flowers are irresistible. Grandeur is far more seductive than mere colour.

Well-bred or Over-bred?
Of course, density is achieved in some shrubs by

their having flowers that have been made larger than nature could manage. There are some perfect examples of this among camellias, some of which annually disappear beneath the wealth of bloom. There may not be more flowers than on a similarly sized bush of the species, but centuries of man's 'improvement' have so greatly enlarged them that they occupy all the available space.

Such shrubs are highly desirable in the main, although some are a bit 'over the top'. *Camellia japonica* 'Drama Girl' has flowers 20cm (8in) wide. They are so heavy that the branches are bent over grotesquely and the whole character of the shrub becomes a mess. The flower density, too, is dissipated. Others, such as 'Alexander Hunter', while never losing their shape, are quite capable of becoming almost completely covered with flowers that touch one another at the edges.

In plants like this, colour is of great importance. A vivid red camellia, maintaining its shape and thus its flower density, is a major force in the garden in spring. So is a white one. Any rose-pink or red will clash violently with 'Debbie', a camellia that was born to be admired in isolation, so much blue is there in its pink. The size of the individual flower is what has made the colour so vividly or even disastrously a part of the scene, not so much the colour itself.

If colours can clash, so can styles. It is, to a large extent, Man who has brought this about. You very rarely see incompatible styles of flowers in nature.

A bright alpine meadow – a riot of genera and families with everything from vetches and roses to gentianellas and anemones – is a miracle of harmony. So is the floor of a lowland wood, and even a tropical swamp, rich in the spectacular, maintains a mastery of the mix and match. When garden flowers look wrong together the problem can usually be traced to a juxtaposition of man-made, formal flowers and nature's informalilty.

Formality in flowers is usually a matter of doubling and breeding for more doubling. It is not always so; the stiffly upright drumsticks of *Primula denticulata* consist of single flowers and were not made by man. However, bathing-cap rhododendrons, camellias with flowers like gymkhana rosettes and roses that ape the toppings on ice-cream sundaes cannot be expected to do other than clash with the simple trumpets, bells, funnels and chalices into which nature fashions so many of her flowers with artless perfection.

When you are working out your planting plans, whether you subscribe to the virtues of related planting or not, you will run into trouble if you fail to take style into consideration. You may have achieved the ultimate in subtlety with foliage, your disposition of shapes may have been inspirational in its cunning, and your appreciation of the beauties of bark and stem second to none. Mix formal with informal, artificial with natural, and you will be like

When garden flowers look wrong together the problem can usually be traced to a juxtaposition of man-made, formal flowers and nature's informality. . . you will run into trouble if you fail to take style into consideration

the lady who wore curlers with her best Balenciaga – well dressed but not quite right somehow.

When all is said and done, there are thousands of colourful shrubs and hundreds of flowering trees from which you can choose. So why fall for red? Or a particular shade of pink? If the plant that you are thinking of buying has ordinary leaves, no autumn colour, a dumpy shape, no discernible elegance of structure, grey-brown, wrinkled bark and brilliant red flowers in May, leave it. Colour isn't everything.

Spring: pyracanthas in flower in the Botanic Garden of Leiden University, Holland

BERRIES AND OTHER FRUIT

If you say, 'Fruit' to a layman – you or me for example – the images that come to mind will be of juicy nectarines, apples and pears, or paw-paws and custard-apples, depending on the individual. To a botanist, though, a fruit is the part or parts of a flower or flower cluster that undergo changes after the flower is fertilised.

Botanically, fruits can be 'true' or 'false'. It is interesting to note that such arcana as capsules, follicles, siliquae and pyxidia are true fruits, whereas apples, figs, strawberries, mulberries and pineapples are false. Among other words allocated to types of fruits are achene, cypsela, carcerule, samara . . . and nut.

As far as gardeners are concerned, fruits are all the bright, dangly things that look pretty and contain seeds, whether they are edible or not. Many trees and shrubs have attractive fruits, and their ornamental use in the garden is something to which we should pay more attention.

Oddly enough, gardeners are loth to plant trees or shrubs just for the ornamental value of their fruit, and they are quite right. A very few plants have displays of berries so long-lasting and vivid that they can stand alone, and even they are notable for their flowering.

What the gardener needs is a wider awareness of the possibilities that exist for exploiting the fruits that last longest and thus have the greatest impact on the gardening year

Pyracanthas, for instance, put on a fine show in spring, especially when planted in poor soils on sunny walls, with dense clouds of small, snowy blossoms. The ensuing berries, especially those in the orange and yellow range, last for months, right through autumn and winter and sometimes into the early part of the following spring. Many cotoneasters, again when given short commons, seem to cover themselves with tiny, white dog roses before donning their well-known cloaks of brilliant berries.

Crab apples, too, make superb floral displays in spring, often outdoing the more renowned cherries. Their fruits, shinily, prominently red or chubbily gold are endearing in their boldness and many have good autumn foliage colour. Hawthorns, especially the pink- and red-flowered ones, are good value and so, of course, are female hollies.

All these are well known and come easily to the mind of the gardener for whom the special, aesthetic meaning of 'fruit' – neither botanical nor gastronomic – has been recognised. The hips of shrub roses are fruit and so are the pendent baubles of many euonymus, but these are well known, too. What the gardener needs is a wider awareness of the possibilities that exist for exploiting the fruits that last longest and thus have the greatest impact on the gardening year.

Pyracantha berries are eminently long lived. However, the red ones disappear first. This is largely because birds are attracted to red berries before any others. In the green and blue world of our planet, red fruits say, 'Come and get me, I'm ripe and juicy and I want you to eat me so that you carry my seed in your gut and thus do a good job of distributing it widely'. Orange works less well, yellow even less, and white berries hang around longest of all – in general, that is. There are always exceptions.

Autumn: pyracanthas in berry on an old cottage in Dorset, England

Sorbus vilmorinii in late summer

In Britain and Ireland the native mountain ash has berries of brilliant scarlet. They last a couple of weeks. Near my house, fat, handsome thrushes gobble them up like orphans in a sweet shop. There would be little point in planting the species as a tree for ornamental berries unless you could hire a squadron of flying cats. Yet there are mountain ashes that are superb for the purpose.

Sorbus 'Joseph Rock', for example, has light yellow berries that deepen to amber. They last long after the fall of the beautifully coloured autumn leaves and strike an unusual note when displayed on the sharply ascending branches. The finely pinnate leaves are beautiful throughout spring and summer, too. *S. vilmorinii*, a most delightful, ferny, small

Sorbus hupehensis. . . *feathery of foliage and with more than a hint of blue in its leaf, turns in autumn as hotly red as a shy damsel receiving a proposition*

tree, manages to keep its berries from late summer, when they are deep maroon, through autumn, during which they fade to pink and onward to white with a pink flush, in which state they stay on into winter. Mind you, not all the berries do this; some stay red and are eaten early, while the latest are eventually made a meal of, but only when the birds are desperate. In this way nature ensures that the seed is distributed over a long period, thus increas-ing its chances of finding the most advantageous germination sites.

Sorbus hupehensis goes about it differently, hanging its berries out like white marbles, and then allowing them to become slightly blushed with purplish pink. This wonderful garden tree, feathery of foliage and with more than a hint of blue in its leaf, turns in autumn as hotly red as a shy damsel receiving a proposition. After shedding its leaves the change in character is astonishing; the bare branches, adrip with snowy baubles, present as cool a face as that of an ice maiden who has heard it all before.

Among the hawthorns, some are more lasting than others. *Crataegus* × *lavallei* seems to be possessed of an obstinate streak; it refuses to drop its deep green leaves until the shortest days of the year and keeps its warm orange berries for a considerable time after them. *C. durobrivensis*, a shrub that is becoming rarer in gardens, has flowers almost an inch across and persistent, deep red berries.

Malus 'Red Jade', which is a small, weeping crab apple, and *M.* 'Red Sentinel' are among the exceptions to the rule that red berries have the shortest lives. They can both be counted on to stay in fruit for many weeks, but you should not expect crabs the size of those on 'John Downie' or any of the many bred for jelly making. For the maximum impact in the garden you are looking for long-lasting ornament and the trees should not be compared with so-called 'fruiting' crab apples, but judged in the arena of general garden excellence.

The exceptions to the rule that you should seek out the berries with the longest tenure are the shrubs whose fruits are so coloured, so prolifically borne, or so well balanced by the plant's performance during the rest of the year that they demand special attention even though they may not be around for so long. One such is *Callicarpa bodinieri giraldii*, of which a clone appears recently to have been selected and called 'Profusion'. This smallish shrub has foliage in which a metallic, purple-bronze seems to lie beneath the surface green. In summer it flowers profusely, with small blossoms of a unique blue-violet, again with a metallic sheen. The berries that follow are like small ball-bearings that look, for all the world, as if made from lilac steel. The colour is impossible to describe properly and has to be seen. Finally, the foliage deepens to true purple before falling.

From the warty, red sausages of magnolias and the big, fat ones of the climber *Akebia quinata*, whose metallic sky-blue astonishes in mild gardens, to the unbelievably persistent, brilliant scarlet berries of *Skimmia reevesiana*, ornamental fruits bring a new dimension to the garden. Most of us under-exploit it, but for all that the constant caveat applies here just as much as anywhere; don't let it get out of proportion.

INTANGIBLES

Without some quality of carriage, elegance, grace, presence, dignity, piquancy or charm, if devoid of any trace of the majestic, imposing, dramatic, aristocratic or impressive, a tree or shrub can try as hard as it likes in other directions and it will fail, as surely as a monkey in a business suit.

Prunus 'Kanzan' may have the flowers, *Symphoricarpos albus* the white berries, *Hippophae rhamnoides* berries and silver-grey foliage, and *Stephanandra incisa* the autumn colour, but none has the stamp of quality that distinguishes a first-class plant. It is difficult to pin down just what it is about a plant that makes this kind of difference. The task is much easier when you attempt to define those aspects that are positively detrimental to the attainment of quality. Dumpiness is a fairly concrete term. There is no mistaking a dumpy shrub – rotund, plain, of displeasing proportions, with no saving grace in the shape of leaves, and with no discernible structure. What is the opposite of dumpiness? The answer turns us back again into the intangible; into the realm of elegance, grace, and so on.

Will, then, a tree or shrub with a definite and visible branch structure come up to scratch? Not necessarily. The common elder looks decidedly common at any time of the year, its branches a higgledy-piggledy network of coarse limbs and misdirected offshoots. You may love its exuberant flowering

You cannot, after all, march into a garden centre and demand of the staff that they provide you with a piquant tree or one that is charismatic

the year after a hot summer and hanker after the wine from its berries, but you cannot, by any means, commend it for its form.

How would you describe a fig in intangible terms? It fits both the literal and the figurative meanings of 'exotic' when in leaf – it is both foreign and redolent of romantic places – but in winter it is stark, sparse and forbidding. 'Graceless' says it all.

In order to convey to you the importance of intangible qualities the only resort is to examples. It is worthless to adjure you to seek out plants that have certain abstract attractions. You cannot, after all, march into a garden centre and demand of the staff that they provide you with a piquant tree or one that is charismatic. Well, you can, but I don't advise it.

Once again, it is a matter of taking every opportunity to see well-grown examples in parks and gardens. Once you have seen the gnarled, buttressed, corky trunk of a seed-raised dawn redwood (those from cuttings are not the same), you will understand what is meant when someone describes it as looking as if it had only just been transplanted from the primeval forests of dinosaur-time. If you have seen one you will know just what they mean; if you have not you will probably think they were writing just after lunch. The fact is that *Metasequoia glyptostroboides* does date from that era and was until the 1940s entirely unknown save from fossils in coal measures. If you bear in mind that no cultivated tree anywhere is sixty years old, and that all except the youngest and those grown from cuttings look inconceivably ancient, you will begin to understand (if you do not already) that intangible qualities are not just important but are the essence of a plant's being.

Viburnum plicatum 'Mariesii' has a definite branch structure and flat heads of white flowers. A mere glance is enough to see that it has the qualities that a common elder, for example, lacks

Go and spend some time in the company of an oak – an 'English' oak, *Quercus robur*. Do not just look at it; sit under it and let it work its magic on you. After a while, the might of its age will begin to tell. You will notice the rugged, essentially reliable, load-bearing strength of its main branches. The way in which sunlight plays through its foliage – gold where there are only green leaves – will fascinate and soothe at the same time. Gradually, you will feel the personality of the great tree and you

will feel safe, protected and peaceful. You may well walk away, 'Modern Citizen' brain in charge again, and think, 'Well, that was a bit silly', but one day you will be back for more.

Few of us are lucky enough to have the space in which to grow large oaks, but that is not the point. Plants have, for want of a better word, personalities, and we will be better gardeners if we accept that and choose our plants accordingly. It is not soft sentimentalism but a recognition of the fact that plants are among the living things with which we share our planet. It may seem anthropomorphic to ascribe to plants characteristics we see in our fellow humans, but it is entirely natural and usually accurate. We can be too urbane and sophisticated sometimes and tempted to scorn our 'Old Adam' judgements.

Pushed into a corner and threatened with dire penalties for failure, one could, perhaps, draw up some general principles that underlie the more abstract attractions of woody plants. Symmetry comes into it; nothing is beautiful if it is ungainly and lop-sided, but proportion is more crucial. The elder fails the test because its branches are tiring to look at. The eye, travelling along a branch, is continually distracted because there is nothing to make it travel smoothly and there are too many bumps and inconsequential changes of direction. A bamboo, such as *Arundinaria nitida*, on the other hand, sweeps your eye up from ground level and smoothly over the curve at the top, to follow it down to the ground-brushing leaf tips. The canes are perfectly tapered so that it is hard to resist their demand for attention.

Salix matsudana 'Tortuosa' is a willow with widely set leaf joints (nodes). For some reason, one side of the stem grows faster than the other between each pair of nodes. However, what gives the tree its strange, contorted look is the fact that the side with the faster growth changes with every node. The result is that each branch is wavy. You might expect the eye to be distracted, but it is not; it follows the waves quite happily and finds the effect of a much-branched tree quite pleasant. It is enabled to do so all year round because the branches are well set apart and the leaves are slender and few.

Contrast this with the other well known contorted tree, *Corylus avellana* 'Contorta'. The twisted hazel looks perfect as a youngster in the nursery in winter, intriguing rather than grotesque. Once in leaf, however, it becomes a dull lump of limp, uninteresting foliage that almost completely hides the branches. Then, as it gets older, it must be cleverly pruned if it is not to become a tiresome, tormented tangle. The catalogue descriptions of the two trees might well be almost identical, while remaining essentially honest; the intangible differences, which would not appear, are so marked as to emerge from the abstract into the concrete.

Our oak may be a battered old stager, veteran of ten-round bouts with heavyweight gales and open-hearted host to teeming, demanding wildlife. It may have lost the odd limb during combat, but there it stands, vastly experienced, like a much-decorated sergeant-major. It is made so by the

steady, upward taper of the massive, short trunk and the strong, sweeping lines as the branches curve upwards from it, with the curve that made its forefathers so perfect for the ribs of Nelson's ships.

Take, by contrast, a certain type of grafted cherry and notice the cylindrical trunk with scarcely any

It is possible, if we take enough trouble, to analyse the intangible attractions of plants, but by so doing we may find ourselves in danger, as it were, of not seeing the wood for the trees

taper at all. It looks like a child's attempt at modelling a tree. At a certain point its trunk abruptly ceases and the branches, rudely straight, radiate outwards as though stuck on with glue. At blossom time it dresses itself in obvious, dangling costume jewellery and embarrasses everyone.

Internodal length has much to do with the abstract effect of a shrub or tree. Foliage consisting of leaves that are too far apart or too close together for their size looks tatty on the one hand or dumpy on the other. Rigidity is another factor; a leaf with a sweetly curving stalk may have the elegance of a ballerina's hand, while another, hanging limply, may look like one element in a mass of dirty washing.

Branch length in proportion to trunk, leaf size as against the overall proportions of the plant, delicacy of line as against crudeness, the ways in which leaves hang or are set on the branchlets, all these give rise to the qualities we recognise in abstract terms. Flowers and fruits, no matter how beautiful they are, will always look 'wrong' if the plant itself is aesthetically a mess. It is possible, if we take enough trouble, to analyse the intangible attractions of plants, but by so doing we may find ourselves in danger, as it were, of not seeing the wood for the trees.

It is probably better to aim for an appreciation of such things based on observation. If you look at shrubs and trees with an eye and mind that are open to beauty, rather than fashion, and which are quickened by simplicity, not elaboration, you will be more than half-way there. The rest comes with practice.

CHAPTER 4

ANNUALS
AND
PERENNIALS

*Rise up, my love, my fair
one, and come away.
For, lo, the winter is past,
the rain is over and gone;
The flowers appear on the
earth; the time of the
singing of birds is come,
and the voice of the turtle
is heard in our land.*

SONG OF SOLOMON 2:10

Annuals and perennials growing together in the sunken
garden at Chenies Manor Garden, Buckinghamshire

Trees and shrubs are fixtures. They change as the year goes by, now leafing up, now flowering, ultimately twiggily bare, but always familiar. Their phases are warmly admired and happily welcomed. Their presence lends stability and creates the essential structure and atmosphere of the garden; they are its walls, pillars, arches and ceiling, and they make us feel comfortable. With them, we have reconstructed the cool, green, restful world of our distant ancestors.

Calmed and reassured by this verdant anodyne, anaesthetised somewhat against the chills and greys of winter, we become receptive to show and drama, hungry for flashiness, anxious to use our dormant facility for reacting swiftly to colours and the messages they carry. In the gloom of the higher latitudes, the darkest days see us preparing gaudily wrapped parcels and happily decorating our houses with a garishness that would be unbearable at any other time. Have you ever taken the Christmas decorations from their boxes in summer and marvelled at their tawdriness?

If only the concept of taste could be magically dismissed from all consideration in gardens! Why not open up joyfully and let the flowers express your love of the year you have been given. . .

Our mortality leads us to some of the most primitive of all our reactions to the natural world. What we also long for in winter is the reassurance that everything will get going again. We need symbols that promise the reawakening of the earth. Not for nothing did religions superimpose themselves upon the rebirth festivals of their predecessors; from Saturnalia to Christmas the prayer is the same – save us from the everlasting dark.

It is not surprising then that we feel deeply pleased as the first noses of green thrust upwards from the slowly warming earth and the pageant of spring and summer commences. Nothing can compare with the fierce annual assertion of the safe arrival of another year. Old Adam rejoices as his senses are assailed by bright colours once again. Modern Citizen takes over, of course, svelte, sophisticated, and admitting nothing more than a

mild delight and the hope that this spring won't be as wet as the last. Up pops last year's experiment in a more adventurous use of colour and the winter-pale cheek flushes with the threat of peer-group rejection. An immediate adjustment is made, the spade with swift deftness obliterating a forgotten resolve towards self expression.

If only the concept of taste could be magically dismissed from all consideration in gardens! Perhaps not just gardens. Is the Pompidou Centre in Paris in good or bad taste? Is downtown Orlando to your taste, or do you find it redolent of Toytown, USA? I like the Miami business district and the Georgian terraces in Brighton. My love of Mozart lives in the same being as a delight in Artie Shaw. I adore the decadent redness of *Dahlia* 'Bishop of Llandaff' and cannot stand dyed carnations. I don't care who knows it, either. Why should you? Why not open up joyfully and let the flowers express your love of the year you have been given – and to blazes with the arbiters of 'taste'.

PLANT OR FLOWER

Perennials are not, of course, entirely to do with flowers. They have other qualities, tangible and intangible, that make them 'good' plants or otherwise in the plantsman's eyes, and many of these qualities are important to the designer, too. The complete gardener will look at the plant as a whole just as readily as he would a tree or shrub.

Nevertheless, with perennials – and certainly with annuals – the flower is what you look at first. Only a handful of perennials, important though they are, and just one or two annuals find a place in the garden solely on account of their foliage, and there are no trunks, branches and barks and precious little autumn colour to consider. So what is it about flowers that distinguishes a worthy member of the garden population from one for which you would not spare the room?

Colour, of course! But please try to look at each colour with your very own eye, not with that of a neighbour, a gardening book, or a censorious guru. Do bright orange kniphofias like 'Fiery Fred' – the name is quite another matter – really deserve the knee-jerk 'Yuck' they usually trigger? They should not be judged by some past history of mixing with the wrong elements, neither should they be con-

No doubt Henry Ford would have approved of *Viola* 'Bowles' Black', especially if mass-produced

demned in isolation. In congenial company they are perfect, statuesque celebrants of midsummer. Certainly the poor things look wildly out of place on the corner patch by the gas station, but so would a benighted, ball-gowned socialite, fuel can in hand, wishing she were back amid the swirling tulle.

If you happen to have a passion for blue, indulge it. If yellow makes you feel cheerful and alleviates your customary quiet, plant lots of it. No colour need be dismissed if it appeals to you, but muddy, impure colours will probably please you much less as time goes by and are best avoided. Similarly, if everyone is 'into' wicked reds and you hate them – leave them out.

This is not to say anything in specific terms about what goes with what – that comes later. For now it is the individual plant and its flowers that concern us. A blue-toned red will clash to most peoples' eyes with one on the yellow side, but the first thing is to decide whether you like blue-reds. If you do not, the question of the clash will not arise, as you will not plant any.

Having decided that you like the colour of a plant's flowers – a purely subjective decision – the next thing is to look objectively at proportion. No matter how wonderful the colour of a flower it will not amount to much if it is small and surrounded by large, uncouth leaves. On the other hand, if there are large numbers of small flowers held well clear of the foliage, the balance may be enough for the plant to be elected. Then again, the foliage itself may be attractive enough to be a longer term asset, or it might expand only after flowering.

Flower Forms

In *Gypsophila* 'Bristol Fairy' the tiny flowers are so numerous and the foliage so unintrusive that it is a first-class plant, particularly where its late-borne inflorescences can take the place previously occupied by the foliage of Oriental poppies. *Thalictrum aquilegifolium* has a perfect combination of cloudy, fluffy heads of tiny flowers and delightful foliage, for all the world like that of columbines. *Brunnera macrophylla* sprays little forget-me-nots lavishly about before its large, round, imposing leaves fully unfurl, and then becomes a foliage plant, spotted and splashed, in some forms, with silver.

Small flowers in small numbers are less than imposing when borne on long, stout stems. They are much more effective when the stems are short, and tiny flowers, which would be merely weedy in a tall plant, take on distinction and dramatic force when stemless or nearly so. Alpine gardeners find border plants coarse in general. Most of their charges have reduced flower stems as a defence against the harsh, gritty winds that would otherwise batter them in the mountains. The alpine specialist's eye, used to flowers that are truly enormous for the sizes of the plants, and given to prizing foliage that is reduced to cushions of the consistency of prickly velvet, rejects the proportions of even the good herbaceous perennials as uncouth. However, I can vouch for the fact that despecialisation restores perspective without destroying the delight in the miniature, and that the proportions of our best border plants are about as ideal as can be selected or achieved.

The shape of a flower is all important. Flowers have dynamic effects on us of two distinct kinds. On the one hand they may attract us closely toward them, so that we end up compulsively examining them at close quarters; on the other they may display showily, demanding that we appreciate them from a distance. Violets and violas are among the former; michaelmas daisies the latter.

We are not drawn forward to daisy flowers generally, but enjoy them en masse. A single, large daisy is either coarse (some ligularias) or not to be taken seriously (sunflowers). In the main, members of the family Compositae are the better the more flowers they bear. A viola is the more prized the more appealing its individual bloom. Do you remember *Viola* 'Irish Molly' or 'Jackanapes' because of its massed effect or because you wanted to get down on your knees and study its face?

The shapes of flowers and the clusters in which they are borne are all-important when it comes to planting perennials in combination. Individually, it boils down simply to which kinds appeal to you. Some people like the sumptuousness of bearded irises, while others greatly enjoy the simplicity of a linum or a campanula.

The stance, poise and posture of flowers have a profound influence on their suitability, let alone their efficacy. We have already seen a telling example in Chapter 1, in which crocosmias of different kinds demanded different treatments. It is an area in which the factual and the intangible become inextricable; a millimetre more of flower stem

may be enough to divide the captivating from the utterly ravishing, and a few degrees elevation on the mouth of a flower may distinguish the elegant from the obvious.

In general, blatancy in shape or carriage is a disadvantage if it is combined with blatant colouring. A flamboyantly shaped flower, subtly but sensuously coloured, as in the Oncobred irises, will always be a winner. A powerful statement of colour, expressed through the medium of simplicity, will be far more devastating than when combined with floral complication or coarseness – 'Bishop of Llandaff', among the most simple of dahlias but raffish in its sinful redness, is a fine example. Poor Bishop! The only flower in its class for wickedness is the uncomplicated trumpet of a blisteringly red Knaphill azalea called, inevitably, 'Satan'. Perhaps, after all, in discerning this distinction, we have arrived at something alarmingly like a partial definition of taste.

Your choice of perennials will be governed, to a large extent, by their individual flowering periods. Again, one may suggest a fundamental rule. The smaller the garden, the longer the flowering periods of the individual plants should be. With a larger garden you can go more for succession; in a small plot the result of that is all too often a matter of having one plant out at a time.

In general, blatancy in shape or carriage is a disadvantage if it is combined with blatant colouring. A flamboyantly shaped flower, subtly but sensuously coloured, will always be a winner

In a way, the length of the flowering period of a perennial is a different matter from that of a shrub. A perennial is above ground for little more than half the year, whereas a shrub is there all the time. A flowering season of one month with a perennial is perhaps 15 per cent of its annual 'life'; with a shrub it is only 8 per cent. In other words, a month is a long time in summer. This should not deter you, however, from looking for the plants with the longest seasons. Within a species there may be many cultivars and their lengths of flowering may well vary greatly.

FOLIAGE

Apart from flowers, perennials are made up of foliage and flower stems. In many cases there are basal leaves and stem leaves, so foliage is not something to be dismissed lightly. Some plants, not necessarily those you would at first think of as foliage plants, are grown as much for their foliage as for their flowers. Sea hollies, such as *Eryngium planum* and *E.* × *oliverianum*, derive much of their beauty from the steely blue of their stems and particularly of the ruffs of spiky bracts (modified leaves) that lie just below the thistle-like flower heads. With others, such as *E. maritimum*, attention shifts to their intensely grey basal leaves.

Perhaps the most celebrated perennial for leaves is *Acanthus mollis*. Its large, deeply lobed leaves have pleased the eye of civilised man long enough to have inspired the decorations on Corinthian columns, and its pink, foxglove-like flowers come second to them. Even so, it is many a mile behind *Gunnera manicata* when it comes to the majesty and complete dominance over flowers that herbaceous leaves can attain.

It is no good having even the most passing thought about planting this giant unless you have ample space and a really moist site, preferably in part shade and not too cold a spot. Provide these, and you will witness the annual unfurling of mighty sails, up to 2.2m (7ft) across and on stems as much high. They are enormous; wide and slightly lobed like Brobdingnagian rhubarb. Their surfaces are covered with designer stubble; we are indebted to Christopher Lloyd for his describing the sound of one's hand rubbing a gunnera leaf as 'like a giant shaving'. Was it also he who likened their stems to the workings of a Victorian musical box? It is a simile that cannot be bettered, although the tune played would have to be monumental.

The flowers of *Gunnera manicata* are more bizarre than attractive. They skulk about in the lower reaches of the mighty leaf stalks as cylindrical, upright, greenish-brown excrescences like large, redundant flue brushes. The personal lives of such plants are best left private.

Ornamental rhubarbs (*Rheum* species) themselves are fine foliage plants for moist places and can

Gunnera manicata **unfurling its giant leaves in late spring**

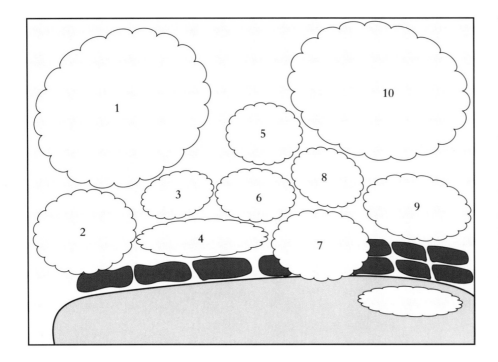

A moist bank beside a large pond

1 *Gunnera manicata* 2 *Hosta sieboldii* 'Elegans'
3 *Peltiphyllum peltatum*
4 *Primula pulverulenta*
5 *Ligularia* 'Desdemona'
6 *Iris pseudacorus* 'Variegata'
7 *Rheum palmatum* 'Bowles' Purple' 8 *Meconopsis grandis*
9 *Lysichitum americanum*
10 *Salix matsudana* 'Tortuosa'

be grown in gardens that are quite small. Moisture, a rich soil and shelter from wind are all they ask and they, too, look fine by water. We should not forget that the waterside is one of the best places to enjoy perennials, nor that most moisture lovers have large leaves.

Evergreen perennials

Among other perennials grown primarily for their foliage are ones that are evergreen. You rarely hear of evergreen perennials. Bergenias figure largely in writings about ground cover, but you do not often see the actual word evergreen applied to them. Others, unaccountably, will be found listed as shrubs. How a phormium (New Zealand flax) can be mistaken for a shrub is something of a mystery. It has no woody structure, but puts forth its sword-like leaves from ground level. Phormiums are magnificent architectural plants; what they have in common with shrubs is that they grow larger year by year and are among the garden's permanent features.

Phormium tenax is a statuesque plant. It makes a 3m (10ft) clump of erect, straight leaves, tapered to points. It is said to need a maritime, mild exposure, but as with most evergreens it is wind that is the enemy. Given shelter it will survive formidable cold, but it is as well to mulch deeply in autumn to prevent the soil's becoming frozen and starving the leaves of water.

There are coloured forms of this species, both purple-leaved and variegated. However, the many brightly striped hybrids between it and the smaller *Phormium cookianum* are not very hardy. They are so striking, however, that there is a case for growing

them in pots and sinking the pots in the garden. Failing that, they are magnificent for tubs and urns that can be brought into protection during the winter.

Bergenias are like mothers-in-law, subject to love and hate on alternate days and never going away. There is something about their large, leathery, rounded leaves that is incongruous. Their propensity for assuming red or bronze tones in winter does nothing to discourage a vision of Bavarian farmers in *lederhosen*, about to do one of

One of the most inspired plantings I have seen consisted simply of a huge clump of **Phormium tenax 'Purpureum'** *sitting in a small lake of bergenias. . . It comprised, in one fell swoop, a garden for all seasons*

those dances where they slap every part of themselves they can reach. Varietal names, such as 'Abendglut' and 'Glockenturm', do not dispel the illusion.

Nevertheless, one of the most inspired plantings I have seen consisted simply of a huge clump of *Phormium tenax* 'Purpureum' sitting in a small lake of bergenias. The contrast in leaf shape was dramatic, the lettuce green of the bergenias against the smoky mahogany of the phormium, a perfect complement, and the reds and pinks of the bergenia flowers picked out, in spring, the red that always underlies this phormium's modest tones. It comprised, in one fell swoop, a garden for all seasons.

If you can find a raison d'être for bergenias, they can contribute vitally to the impact of a planting. Just plant them for their own sake though, and you bring on the clowns. They need the company of other evergreens and the bolder the better.

Hostas

There is a sort of sliding scale that applies to the proportional importance of foliage and flowers in non-woody plants. At one end are gunneras, while at the other are the many annuals for whose foliage we spare little thought and whose flowers are paramount.

Quite close to the leafy end of the scale are the hostas. These much-vaunted but less-understood plants are grown principally for their foliage but, in many cases, have flowers quite as handsome as those of other plants whose leaves are not particularly attractive. There tend to be fashions in hostas. For a few years they are the thing to be seen growing, unusual varieties penetrate the garden centres and they become the sweethearts of the gardening media. Next, a flood of varieties arrives, many bearing names more appropriate to inhabitants of Disney World, and the cognoscenti give them the big cold shoulder, 'But darling, everyone's growing hostas these days!'

Fashion in plants is truly destructive. As has happened so often before with ferns, violas, double primroses and many more, once the social back is turned on a group of plants, the baby is gone with the bath water. One can only hope that hostas (and hemerocallis, which for some obscure reason share a Society with them) will not suffer the same fate. You may not think names like 'Big Daddy', 'Blue Piecrust' or 'Chartreuse Wiggles' (no kidding) are music to the ear, but there is no denying the beauty of hostas and we do not want to lose them. I fear the danger is real, however, if there are many more like 'Zounds', 'Ryan's Big One' and 'Green Sheen'. 'Zounds', by the way, is also the name of a bearded iris, among whose ilk may be found 'Winkieland',· 'Wow' and 'Zipper'. *Sic transit . . .*

The most common misconception about hostas is that they need shade. They do not. What they must have is moisture, not in copious amounts, but steadily delivered at the roots. This means one thing: a highly vegetable soil with good drainage. The more organic matter a soil contains, the more it will retain moisture. It must however, be well oxygenated, and this means that it must also be well

Blue-grey and variegated hostas, accentuated by association with *Heuchera* 'Palace Purple'

drained. Half the volume of a good soil is empty space – air – and if it is full of water a toxic, anaerobic environment ensues which gardeners call 'sour'.

Hostas like 'Honey Bells' – which has honey-coloured leaves, if that has anything to do with it – look much better where they receive sun for a good part of the day. Scorching is a danger with hostas, it's true, especially with those variegated in white, but yellow-leaved ones do not seem nearly as susceptible. What sun does for this variety, as it does for others whose leaves tend to overlap, is to make it grow in a more compact way so that the leaves become neatly imbricated like tiles on a roof. Come to think of it, hosta-shaped shingles would be most attractive.

Hosta 'Honey Bells'

GRASSES, SEDGES AND FERNS

Just where grasses fit into the gardener's scheme of things varies according to whom you consult. There are attempts from time to time to make something cultish of them and then there is a great debate as to what category they fit. I think the best thing is to regard them as perennials at the leafy end of the scale and let the botanical distinctions go hang. Treat grasses like plants, de-categorise them, and you will find yourself enjoying their swishy movement and the linear accent they strike.

Grasses are everything from bamboos to lawn fescues. They do not technically include sedges, which belong to the family Cyperaceae, whereas grasses and bamboos comprise the Graminae.

Treat grasses like plants, de-categorise them, and you will find yourself enjoying their swishy movement and the linear accent they strike

Sedges have a different structure and the flowers are also different, but as far as foliage effect goes they are in the same gardening strand.

The finest sedge is *Carex stricta* 'Bowles' Golden', which makes a 60cm (2ft) fountain of rough, slender, arching leaves that become golden yellow at the beginning of summer and do not fade until it is over. It can be slow to establish, but is a fixture once its feet are well under the table. It is a most striking and effective contrast to hostas with green or blue foliage and likes just the same conditions. The combination is a classic example of synergy, in which each partner is more impressive than when on its own.

Carex morrowii 'Evergold' is a small sedge, not much more than 20cm (8in) in height, whose foliage is longitudinally variegated in green and gold. It is ideal for small gardens and makes a striking contrast when paired with 'Blue Glow', a first-class selection of *Festuca glauca* with intensely blue-silver leaves.

The taller grasses make very strong statements about linear, often arching foliage, feathery flower heads, and different sorts of home environment from their non-grassy neighbours. They should be used sparingly. The idea is to relate the grasses one to another across the intervening spaces without necessarily relating them to the other plants in those spaces. You create a grass theme that stands out from everything else. It is easy to overdo this and then the contrast, which is what it is all about, is lost.

Unfortunately, the grass you almost always see is the pampas grass, *Cortaderia selloana*, in one of its forms. Full many a small garden is stuck with a huge, overbearing clump of 3m (10ft) or so, which goes off like a mighty firework for a month in autumn and then spends the rest of the year cutting the children's hands to bits. The two great land-grabbing bandits of suburban real estate are the weeping willow and the ubiquitous pampas grass. They deserve each other.

Lovely grasses like *Miscanthus sinensis* 'Zebrinus', whose straight leaves become striped across with

Grasses relate best one to another. That having been said, they do little for one another when planted all together in a 'grassery'

yellow, and whose feathery, tan flower heads defy the chills of autumn, or the less tall *Helictotrichon sempervirens*, at 1.2m (4ft), blue and erect of leaf but with grey, swaying flower stems, are much more amenable and have the indefinable cachet of 'quality'.

By all means pick up the blue of a grass's leaves and carry it off to be echoed in the foliage of a eucalyptus or *Ruta graveolens* 'Jackman's Blue'. Related planting always works; you cannot spoil anything by carrying it out. Grasses, however, relate best one to another. That having been said, they do little for one another when planted all together in a 'grassery'. Unless you are a collector of grasses, this is best avoided as it can soon look tatty and the individual charms of the inhabitants become lost in the mass.

This is especially so during winter, when the flowering stems of grasses make considerable ornamental features. Clustered together, there is a considerable danger of untidiness, but when the rest of the garden is tidy and the grasses are well separated, their feathery stems, curved under the weight of moisture or filigreed with frost, are most fetching.

Bamboos

Bamboos belong in larger gardens. There are some little ones just 30-60cm (1-2ft) high but they have little impact. Non-invasive bamboos such as *Arundinaria nitida*, on the other hand, add greatly to the character of a garden. This species makes wide clumps of slender, flexible canes with neat, short, linear leaves. The outer canes sweep over so that the tips just touch the ground, making a bower in which it is not only children who love to hide. *A. murielae* is similar.

Apart from one or two others – *Arundinaria viridistriata*, whose brightly gold-striped leaves are an excellent, all-year focus of brightness, and the broad-leaved, short-caned *Shibataea kumasasa*, which loves a moist spot – that is as far as one dares to go with recommending bamboos without risking the wrath to come. They are, on the whole, plants to approach with great wariness.

The title of this book is *Plants With Impact* and it is not fair to avoid mentioning those whose impact might well be disastrous. Here there is no escaping the fact that many bamboos are pugnaciously invasive, capable of mounting a blitzkrieg of overwhelming proportions. *Sasa palmata*, for instance, a lovely bamboo of some 2m (6ft) with leaves like large spearheads, makes couch grass and other rhizomatous invaders of pastureland and gardens look like vegetable pussy cats.

Once in, bamboos are the devil to get out. Their roots and stem bases make mats like chain-mail. My crew found it necessary to use a forester's

Festuca glauca forming part of an association of plants with blue-grey foliage. This subtle but fairly monochrome arrangement would benefit from the addition of a small, yellow-leaved sedge such as *Carex morrowii* 'Evergold' as a contrasting accent

winch, designed for hauling large tree stumps bodily out of the ground, to persuade bamboos to give up their hold on the earth, and these were not runners, but the peaceful *Arundinaria japonica*. The problem was that the species had flowered for several years running, as it did all over the world in those same years, and was flowering itself to death. Bamboos do not always die after flowering, but often do, and certainly perish if repeat flowering takes over. Nobody knows why they flower when

Nobody knows why they flower when they do; your bamboo may not flower in your lifetime, but then it might just do so a few years after you plant it. It might survive, but then it might not, and I defy you to dig it out

they do; your bamboo may not flower in your lifetime, but then it might just do so a few years after you plant it. It might survive, but then it might not and I defy you to dig it out.

Some years ago I visited a garden that used to be owned by a dedicated and highly knowledgeable collector of bamboos. The visit was in order to assess the national importance of the collection and advise the folk who had inherited it. It was a salutary lesson. Many species had died, leaving cane stubble many yards across in a number of cases. It would have taken much labour, heavy machinery, and a complete replanting to have brought that garden back to being a pleasurable place again.

In Praise of Ferns

Ferns are a different proposition altogether, a neglected group of plants whose virtues deserve to be sung loud and long. The very adjective 'ferny' is a word of praise when applied to anything else, yet ferns are barely regarded as garden plants at all. What a shame this is! Perhaps it is still a reaction to the gloom that pervaded the fern plantings of the Victorians; more likely it is a reflection of the public's view of ferns as weeds – bracken in various guises.

Ferns are marvellous companions for other plants. Their green fronds can hide the bare lower limbs of elderly shrubs, show off contrasting, boldly entire leaves like the round, maroon-backed foliage of *Ligularia* 'Desdemona', and act as a foil for flowers (including the ligularia's) in moist, semishady places. Not that they should be banished to the nether darkness; in fact, they will probably do badly there. Ferns do tend to be relegated to the rubbish corners of gardens. 'What shall we do with this bit?' 'I know, let's make a rockery or grow ferns or something.' Ferns are plants just like any others and deserve to have their case reviewed and to be released on the grounds of false prosecution.

Until you have seen the bright gloss on the undulating, strap-shaped fronds of the hart's tongue, *Asplenium scolopendrium*, glittering in winter at the upstart snowdrops, or witnessed the quiet majesty of *Osmunda regalis*, the royal fern, at the waterside in summer, you may well be forgiven for dismissing ferns as 'bracken'. A sight of the upright, neatly symmetrical, crested, laddery fronds of *Dryopteris affinis* 'The King' erupting out of a sea of *Geranium endressii*, will go a long way towards converting you and will soon have you marvelling at the perfect shuttlecocks of *Matteuccia struthiopteris*, nobly decorating your moist area among trees. You will start to hanker after the Japanese painted fern, the American oak fern, and even, if your garden is mild, the Australian tree fern. However, when this stage is reached you will be in grave danger, for beyond lies the slippery descent into becoming a true lover of ferns, beyond which lies the uncharted world of the pteridologist – fern freak to you and me.

Ferns should be regarded in the same light as any other foliage plants. Whether they are large ones in a border or small ones among the crevices of the rock garden, try if you can to look at them just as plants with lovely leaves. Yes, they are fronds, but so what? Ferns, more than any other plants, are locked into the categorisation we are trying to get away from. Luckily, there is a movement towards growing them happily among other plants – scattered among the shrubs and peeping prettily among the perennials. They find the shelter, shade and moisture they need when in good company, and reward gardeners by enriching the palette of green and promoting the pageant of shape and form to a panoply.

FOLIAGE AND FLOWERS

If you have ever studied physics – even if you have struggled manfully for a while only to leave it behind for ever with a sigh of relief – you will be sure to remember the phrase, 'All things being equal'. What it meant was that, in order to isolate a set of phenomena and make calculations about them, you had to ignore other things that were happening, such as friction or air resistance. This, however, did not invalidate your calculations.

The point we have reached is where you are gently to be told that related planting is subject to 'all things being equal'. Certain factors have been left out, which can now be added, but they do not invalidate the concept. Your garden will be very much the stronger and more harmonious if it is planted so that the major plants and boldest plantings relate to one another, but it will lack something if other factors are ignored.

These come under the blanket heading of 'flair' and are intangible. Gardeners, like plants, have concrete and abstract qualities; among the former may be the ability to produce asparagus of melting tenderness, while the latter may include an unerring eye for unusual, seemingly illogical, but effective plant combinations. To plan ·and plant a garden according to the principles of related planting is to create a harmonious garden without necessarily being possessed of any flair at all. Where the magic comes in is where individual 'feel' and instinct are brought into play.

The royal fern, *Osmunda regalis*, thrives in wet positions. Its fronds turn the colour of spun gold in autumn. It is found wild in many parts of the world, including North America but, although abundant in the west of Ireland, collection of its roots for their fibre has almost eliminated it from England

The unconscious mind is, after all, only the Old Adam emerging from beneath the blanket of Modern Citizenry. When the two work together and a discipline is superimposed on the unconscious, design principles and flair can live together and work in tandem to produce what, I suppose, must be called 'art'.

When it comes to planting perennials and annuals in which the roles of foliage and shapes become increasingly subordinate to colour, success becomes more and more dependent on artistic sensitivity. There are still principles at work, but instinctive understanding becomes more necessary. The combination of plantsmanship and design flair that we are seeking takes on a vital importance.

Further along the sliding scale of proportion between flowers and leaves than those grown primarily for their foliage are the very many whose leaves are almost as important as their flowers. Sometimes, in fact, they are just as important, but the relationship varies with how they appear in different situations.

Planting in Practice
If this seems as clear as mud, try an example. *Iris sibirica* is a plant of some 90cm (3ft) high, with long,

narrow, upright, almost grassy leaves. For much of the summer it carries its flowers in shades of blue, white or cream on stems just a little longer than the leaves. Now, imagine a large colony of a white-flowered form on the bank of a pond made in the natural style. Not far away, in the very shallow water, *Iris pseudacorus* 'Variegata' bears yellow flags

It is all too easy to become too prissily plantsmanlike or too unheedingly colour-oriented. It is easy, too, to adopt what can only be described as a snobbish attitude towards annuals

over handsomely gold-striped, more stiffly erect leaves, now fading slightly to green. Across the pond, one of the less invasive bulrushes emphasises the vertical accents, while its neighbour, *Zantedeschia aethiopica*, the arum lily, echoes and majestically magnifies the purity of the Siberian iris's blooms.

This is related planting. The leaves of the Siberian

iris are important to the statement about strong, upright, linear leaves and, by their contrasting greenness, draw attention to the striped ones of the other iris. Its white flowers are essential to the exchange of messages with the arum lily. Thus the leaves and flowers play equally important parts.

Now imagine the same iris in a closely planted herbaceous border. It is surrounded by colour, a patch of white designed here to emphasise the blues of campanulas and there the pinks and reds of phloxes. The full blaze of midsummer has taken over the border, and beyond are brilliant red pyrethrums, yellow day-lilies and another phlox – white this time – *Phlox paniculata* 'Fujiyama'.

It does not take much thought to realise that in this scenario the leaves of the iris are a secondary consideration and that it is its flowers that count for more. They are fulfilling the designer's intentions by acting as a foil for some neighbours and as a link

Zantedeschia aethiopica 'Crowborough' in the company of rodgersias and *Lobelia tupa*, whose deep red spikes, here in tight bud, will bring a new dimension to the planting. The foliage component, with its contrasting but complementary shapes, is as important to the beauty of the group as the flowers

to others, but the leaves are of lesser moment. They still play a part, however, in the harmony and cohesion of the border. It is at this stage that it is all too easy to tip too far either way; to become too prissily plantsmanlike or too unheedingly colour-oriented.

It is easy, too, to adopt what can only be described as a snobbish attitude towards annuals. Whether they are hardy annuals, sown where they are to grow, or half-hardy annuals sown and raised in heat, they are still plants and it does not make the slightest difference what sort they are when it comes to how they look in company.

You rarely find the foliage of annuals being given a second's thought, yet there are many that are as handsome as anything in the collections of the most ardent plantsmen. *Ricinus communis*, the castor oil plant, has magnificent, palmate leaves in deep brown-bronze or bronzed carmine. Among strong red flowers of whatever persuasion it is perfectly in keeping and is no mean foil for the large, glossy, green leaves of *Fatsia japonica*, which is a hardy shrub. And yet how often do you hear of its being recommended for the mixed border?

Amaranthus hypochondriacus (the specific epithet

You rarely find the foliage of annuals being given a second's thought, yet there are many that are as handsome as anything in the collections of the most ardent plantsmen

means 'of melancholy appearance', referring to its dusky flowers) is the hardy annual, called prince's feather, whose reddish-green leaves have a metallic sheen. It is the perfect complement to artemisias, with both its foliage and the upright plumes of dark crimson flowers contrasting wonderfully with the silver filigree of its companions.

The foliage of annuals does not have to be bold or differently coloured in order to be highly effective. Nigellas are fascinating near the front of the border when their rounded flowers try unsuccessfully to hide behind the flimsy, delicately traced network of filaments that create the love-in-a-mist illusion. The plain green of the neatly-cut leaves of *Nemophila insignis* gives it much of its appeal, acting

as a perfectly toned-in background for the soft blue, white-centred flowers. And red, pink and white cosmos have a character all of their own, lent to them by their ferny foliage, so finely divided as to remind one of candyfloss.

PERENNIALS IN SHADE

If you had two people sharing a garden, one of whom was good at related planting and the other of whom had a dashing, artistic way with colour, to deal with perennials by giving responsibility for planting in shade to the former and in sun to the latter would be the perfect division of labour.

The reason for this is that, in general, plants whose natural habitat is shady, or which come from places where the soil and atmosphere are moist, tend to have evolved large leaves. The hotter and drier the natural environment, the smaller the leaves become until, in extreme cases, they disappear altogether, as in some African acacias and the cactuses. It follows that a shady part of the garden will become inhabited by leafy plants, while those in sun will be grown mainly for their flowers.

In shade, the predominance of leaf form will dictate the relationships between plants. There is an essential informality in shade plantings, brought about by their very leafiness. It is neither easy nor natural to try to make formal arrangments of plants with large leaves, and a well executed shade planting is always characterised by a sort of orderly casualness.

Flowers are important, of course, but shade lovers tend to be at the leafy end of the sliding scale of leaf-to-flower proportions, and foliage will often come out on top. When it does not, it is an indication that the plants love shade only in cultivation; in the wild they are likely to live where the soil is wet but where they receive plenty of sunshine.

One way of approaching the planning of a shade planting is first to establish what are going to be the major, structural plants. In this context it does not mean the woody plants, as in most gardens it is they that will be creating the shade in the first place, or certainly increasing its amount, but the large perennials, such as rheums, lysichitums, *Osmunda regalis*, rodgersias and even gunnera. These are the plants that will determine the fundamental character of one sort of shade planting.

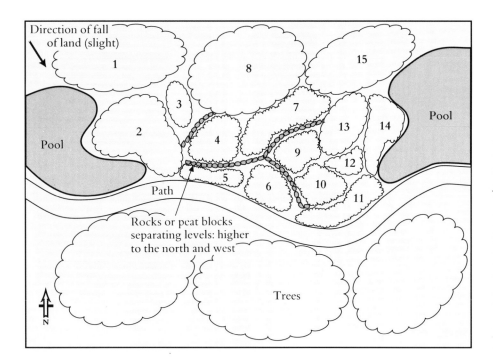

Direction of fall
of land (slight)

1

8

15

3

7

2

4

13

14

Pool

9

12

5

6

10

Pool

11

Path

Rocks or peat blocks
separating levels: higher
to the north and west

Trees

N

1 *Lysichitum americanum*
2 *Osmunda regalis* (Royal
Fern) 3 *Primula pulverulenta*
4 *Primula bulleyana* 5 *Primula
farinosa* 6 *Primula vulgaris*
7 *Meconopsis grandis* 8
Matteuccia struthiopteris
(Shuttlecock Fern)
9 *Asplenium scolopendrium*
(Hart's Tongue Fern)
10 *Meconopsis betonicifolia*
'Alba' 11 *Meconopsis
betonicifolia* 12 *Trillium
chloropetalum* 13 *Ligularia
'Desdemona'* 14 *Primula
florindae* 15 *Rodgersia
aesculifolia*

**An informal planting in shade, demonstrating leafiness
and block planting**

With the other sort, which might, for want of a
better word, be called 'glade planting', there are no
dominant perennials such as these, but the shady
area is broken up by paths or grassy areas into informal beds, where smaller perennials, such as
primulas, meconopsis, anemones and ferns can be
allowed to establish a more faerie atmosphere of the
sort more familiar in a temperate woodland. Informality will still impose itself, however.

Shade plantings in the style perfected at the Royal
Botanic Garden, Edinburgh, are among the most
effective of all. They are essentially informal, but
there is a discipline about them, a kind of horticultural excellence, that we might all copy to great
advantage, while scaling things down to what our
individual gardens will allow.

The major, structural perennials are given full
sway. In a small garden you might have room only
for one or two small groups of rodgersia or
ligularia, but that does not matter; the system
works just the same. Between and among the larger
plants, smaller ones whose flower power is greater
are block-planted, the blocks being given informal
shapes. They may be contiguous or separated by
rockwork, stepping stones or even peat blocks.

Primulas
Primulas are perfect subjects for this kind of treatment. The primula season is a long one, there are
many floriferous species that love a shady, moist
place, and their foliage is usually bold and attractive
after the flowers have faded.

In a small garden it is preferable, as usual, to look
for the plants that will afford the longest season of
flower, but the temptation to create spottiness by
trying to have your cake and eat it should be
resisted. Four groups of six primulas are effective;
twenty-four different ones are a mess.

The primrose types are the primulas of spring.
Many of them are mountain plants and belong as
single specimens in rock garden crevices, where
their effectiveness is a function of the miniature

*It is an axiom that the more casual the
garden appears, the more difficult and time-
consuming it is to maintain*

charm of that environment. Others, such as *Primula
vulgaris* itself and the less artificial, less gaudy
polyanthus, are woodlanders and ideal for the block
planting treatment.

It is simply a matter of obtaining enough plants,
preferably by raising them from seed, and then
planting them at a density which will ensure that
their leaves will just overlap at maturity. Paradoxically for a generally informal planting, they are at
their most effective when planted with an almost
mathematical regularity. The result at flowering
time is a carpet of blossom, and the summer will see
a continuous, weed-smothering covering of green.

By then, the candelabra primulas will be out.
These have stems of between 22 and 90cm (9–36in)
high, at regular intervals on which are whorls of

outward-pointing flowers. There are several species and it is as well to obtain seed that will come true or buy plants, as hybridisation is rife. Mixed candelabra primulas are lovely when scattered about in drifts throughout a large, highly informal planting, but most of us have neither the room nor the time and labour that such gardens demand. It is an axiom that the more casual the garden appears, the more difficult and time consuming it is to maintain.

The most amenable of the candelabras is *Primula pulverulenta*. It is 45-60cm (18-24in) high, sometimes more in cool, moist places. The flowers are rich crimson and the stems are beautifully dusted with a white farina. In the main, asiatic primulas prefer cool climates such as that of Scotland or parts of the coastal areas of northern Oregon and Washington, but this species thrives and seeds itself merrily where it is much warmer, as long as it has a little shade and a moisture-retaining soil. There is a shell pink form called 'Bartley Strain', which is one of the most lovely of all garden plants. From seed, eighty percent or so of the plants will have flowers of the identical pink shade, but the rest will be the usual red of the species. What you do is to plant the lot, and when the red ones show up dig them up ruthlessly and throw them away. You may be advised merely to remove the flower stems and destroy the plants later, but you are sure to forget – most people do.

Candelabra primulas, ferns and water: a wild swamp in miniature. It is entirely natural-looking but is in fact a thoughtful, skilful piece of gardening with each plant in its right place

Primula pulverulenta and Japanese azaleas in Dorset, England. This primula may vary its flowering by as much as two months, depending on latitude, and will not be seen in bloom at the same time as azaleas in colder, more northerly places

Primula bulleyana is another that settles down happily far away from the coolness its brethren seek. Its flowers are more rounded than those of *P. pulverulenta*, and are of a soft yellow that is at variance with the orange that is often ascribed to them. Orange tones creep in when it has crossed with *P. chungensis* or the diminutive, short-lived, *P. cockburniana*. There are several other species but most suffer from coarseness (*P. japonica*) or dowdy colours (*P. beesiana*). Perhaps the very best of all are named hybrids, such as 'Inverewe' and 'Rowallane', whose clear colours and superb stature are worth every penny of their cost and every bit of the effort you might have to expend in finding them.

Really moist, even wet places will support colonies of the primulas often described as giant cowslips. The largest is *P. florindae*. It flowers later than the candelabras and has larger leaves. The stems are up to 90cm (3ft) tall and each one of the several arising from a crown has a terminal cluster of hanging, fragrant bells. They are pale lemon yellow with white powdering and are most elegant. It is one of the Sikkimensis series of primulas, most of which like wetness; as well as being the most perennial it has the longest flowering season, extending often to several weeks.

Primula florindae 'Copper Form', a richly coloured variation on the more usual lemon yellow of the Himalayan giant cowslip

Meconopsis
Primulas and meconopsis go together like needle and thread, but you cannot grow asiatic meconopsis where the soil is calcareous (limy). Enthusiasts derive great pleasure from growing the monocarpic species that flower once and then die, as there are some great beauties both in leaf and flower among

Meconopsis grandis has larger flowers and is a better perennial if it likes you. The blooms are like long-stalked Tiffany lampshades – nature having a try at art deco

them. For most of us, however, it is one of gardening's great joys to grow the blue Himalayan poppies, most of which are perennial. They really must have a leafy or peaty soil with moisture but good drainage, some shade and coolness, and – again – no lime in the soil.

The most commonly grown species is *Meconopsis betonicifolia*, which was called *M. baileyi* for many years, but that was a long time ago and we should be getting our tongues round the 'correct' name by now. It is anything from 60-120cm (2-4ft) tall, depending on conditions, and has big, blue poppy flowers in early summer. The foliage is greyish green and distinctly whiskery. It is easy from seed provided you do not cover the seed at all and do not fail to water at least once at a very early stage with Cheshunt Compound, otherwise the whole lot will collapse with damping-off disease. Meconopsis are not that mad about being perennial and try to get out of it, so the thing to do is to remove incipient flowering stems before they develop. Prevent flowering for a year and the plants hand in their monocarpic cards and start fresh careers as perennials.

Meconopsis grandis has larger flowers and is a better perennial if it likes you. The blooms are like long-stalked Tiffany lampshades – nature having a try at art deco. The blue is variable and tends, as with the last species, to take on mauve tints in drier,

Tiffany lampshades in saxe blue? The bewitching flowers of this form of *Meconopsis grandis* are of the swan-necked, true blue type close to those collected by Sherriff in Tibet

(*Left*) *Trillium grandiflorum*, the Wake Robin of woodland in north-western America (*Right*) *Trillium sessile*. Trilliums enjoy a leafy or peaty soil and prefer shade. The dappled shade cast by trees overhead allows them to be highlighted by occasional shafts of sunlight

warmer districts. The queen of the blue poppies is the hybrid between the two, *M.* × *sheldonii*, and there are forms of this that have been given varietal names; some are better than others but all are magnificent.

Woodland Perennials

Block planting in shade can be carried out with any appropriate plants. Trilliums, the American wood lilies whose leaves and floral parts are all in threes, are highly effective when planted in this way. *Trillium grandiflorum* in particular, which has large, open, white flowers, is ideal and contrasts excitingly with the flat foliage and upright, flame-like petals of *T. sessile* or the taller *T. chloropetalum*.

As with most groups of plants, experiment and study pay dividends. The place to look for information is anywhere you see 'plants for woodland' mentioned. 'Waterside' and such epithets usually sees you well into water lilies and bulrushes. There is no knowing how many of us own woodland – the late Lord Rothschild is reputed to have said that even the smallest garden should have at least ten acres of it – but most of us can create the conditions that are associated with the woodland floor.

You might think glade planting to be the province of the large landowner but, as the song says, 'it ain't necessarily so'. A lawn with trees and large shrubs casting shade on it is a glade as far as plants

are concerned. Informal beds made at intervals along the shade side can be planted with the shade-loving, woodland plants for whom it will be a home from home. Often such beds are made, but left with powdery, poor soil. Sometimes there are rockeries; sad, inappropriate places, slippery in winter and poverty-stricken in summer.

Once again, liberal amounts – no, copious quantities – of organic material are the answer, dug in initially and mulched annually thereafter. Then, instead of gouty saxifrages and arthritic aubrietas there should be Japanese anemones – white 'Honorine Jobert' and the lovely, common pink one called simply *Anemone japonica* – for 120cm (4ft) high, luxuriant displays in autumn. Their handsome, three-lobed foliage is very much of the woodland, as is that of *Kirengeshoma palmata*, whose mysterious, yellow flowers are overcome by shyness if the situation is other than a cool one. It needs a lime-free soil, too.

The smaller gems of the woodland can be given room. . . in a way that suggests the random daintiness of a fairy wood

Here, too is an ideal place for ferns, hostas and bergenias, but the smaller gems of the woodland can be given room, not in block planting, but in a way that suggests the random daintiness of a fairy wood. Wood anemones for spring, bird's eye primroses a bit later. Hellebores, trilliums again – the smaller ones – and even the exquisite double form of the bloodroot, *Sanguinaria canadensis* 'Plena', whose snowy pompoms on short, naked stems are short-lived but so riveting in their purity that to experience them is something that cannot be denied. I travel annually to Wisley to see them, five hundred miles as the 737 flies.

PERENNIALS AND ANNUALS IN SUN

In shady places, where leaves dominate, related planting of perennials helps to promote harmony and balance. What separates the very good from the brilliant, however, is the amount of artistic flair that is brought to bear in creating atmosphere and in using colour in the shady environment. In sun, we have to deal with plants whose flowers are the wage earners, and whose leaves are of much less significance. Of course, there are some that are planted primarily for their foliage, but they are in the minority.

It goes without saying that flowers exert great influences upon us. Most of us love them and revel in their beautiful colours. While we look at how it all works, however, and how the whole thing can break down if we are not careful, we should never lose sight of the fact that flowers will have their greatest impact when associated with an envelope of green.

The subject at the moment is not bulbs, but they are flowers after all and will allow me to illustrate the point. I was privileged, not long ago, to tour Holland as a guest of the International Flowerbulb Centre. One of the visits was to a collection of bulbs of historical importance to the development of modern tulips. I spent quite a long time in the field, which was a dazzling mass of colours, square after oblong after rectangle of reds, pinks, near-blacks, whites, yellows and stripes. It was instructive, but induced a feeling of restlessness and ennui and I left and sat on the lawn by the office building, where some perfectly ordinary shrubs grew. Soon I was able to return to the bulb field, refreshed, the green grass and shrubs having done their job of restoring the balance.

Our inner ancient self will not be denied. You can do what you like in your own garden, but do think twice about filling it with the proverbial 'riot' of colour. We were not made to look at raw colour all the time. We must have green. Our flower-power plants need the coolness and restfulness of green nearby and will be so much the more effective by contrast.

Colour in the Garden
Having established that we are not about to consider colour and flowers in isolation, but with a constant consciousness of the presence of green, we can go on to see how colour works, knowing that, if we become dazzled, we can turn a few pages and restore ourselves with thoughts of verdance, boskage and lettucy leafage.

You may possibly be scratching your head and asking what the Dickens I'm on about, and if you do not have a well developed colour sense I am sure you will be. We are all different, thank goodness, and there must have been some of the tribe who were extra good at spotting bright berries at long distances, others who could tell at a glance that they were not quite ripe, and still others who stayed home and kept the fire going. If you are descended from a long line of fire-keepers, skin-curers and other such essential members of ancient society, you are probably of more value to society than I am but don't know sky-blue-pink from a bull's foot.

Never mind. It's your garden. However, if you are a berry-hunter manqué, whose life has been too busy with the modern equivalents of campfire chores, a quick run round the way colour works may open your Old Adam eye and find you revealed as a gardener, if not quite of Jekyllian flair, then not too far away.

Firstly, it is important to realise that the effect of a colour depends greatly on how much of it is present. A very small patch of geranium-red in a large expanse of white is not all that significant, yet it can make the whole of the white area look quite a lot whiter. Blue will have the same effect, but you will need more of it. Yellow will show up every slightest defect in the white, but it will need a larger amount still of the intruding colour.

Colour clashes largely occur when large masses of incompatible colours are put near or next to one another. The clash is lessened by distraction, as in an alpine hayfield in full flower, when so many individual blobs of different colours occur that clashes do not matter. It is also lessened when one of the colour masses is small but, even so, clashing massed

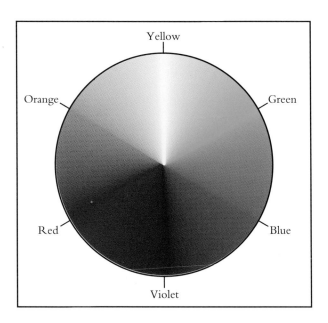

The colour wheel

colours need a buffer between them, which may be of any colour as long as it is entirely different from the two offenders.

You will often hear it said that colours in nature do not clash. This is perfectly true, but you are not dealing with natural effects, you are creating a garden, a place in which the natural is suspended. A garden is a place of artifice, and artifice has its own rules. Colours in the garden most certainly can clash. They can argue, scream at one another, tear each other's eyes out and declare total war. Only the gardener or winter can end hostilities. Colour mismatches are not the end of the world, as you can, in due season, move the plants around and put matters right. However, it is much better to avoid them in the first place.

Theory of Colour

We use the word 'colour' loosely in everyday life, including in it mixtures that are not colours at all. Colours are pure and are the ones you see in a rainbow; red, orange, yellow, green, blue, indigo and violet. Indigo is really a step on the way between blue and violet and hardly warrants a name of its own, so there are six main colours.

They are not, however, distinct, and change very gradually, one into another. Orange becomes

There are almost always several hues present, rather like in a piece of Donegal tweed. . . Our eyes cannot see this with flowers, but it does have an influence on what we can get away with in putting 'colours' together

redder and redder until it is red, and also becomes more and more yellow (less red) until it is yellow. If, instead of a rainbow, you put the colours in a wheel, they merge one into another without a break. This is because they are all parts of the white light that reaches us from the sun. White is the presence or reflection of all of them; black is their total absence or absorption.

The colours we see around us are produced by the absorption and reflection of components of white light. In plants, different pigments absorb and reflect light at different wavelengths; white pigments reflect all wavelengths and black absorbs them. There are usually mixtures of pigments, however, so that you may have a pure colour present, but also black or white. The pure colours are called *hues*. They represent the colours at their maximum intensities, undiluted with black or white. With white added, they become *tints*; Dilution with grey (black plus white) produces *shades*.

The situation where there is one hue plus black or white is one of the famous ones where 'all things are equal'. It ignores the fact that there are almost always several hues present, rather like in a piece of Donegal tweed, which may look soft green from a distance but on close examination is seen to have red, blue, and even orange threads in its weave. Our eye cannot see this with flowers, but it does have an influence on what we can get away with in putting 'colours' together.

Colours in Combination

Pure hues in close juxtaposition influence one another quite profoundly. If you take any one of the three sectors of the colour wheel above, you will find that the secondary hue in the middle – for example, orange – appears to move towards one primary if surrounded by the other. In other words, orange surrounded by red looks more yellow; encircled by yellow it appears to be more red. Green in a field of blue seems more yellow; in the middle of yellow it is bluer. Violet shifts towards red – quite dramatically so – when surrounded by blue, and when in the midst of red it almost becomes indigo.

The effect is the same when the two hues are placed next to one another, although you need a better eye to see it than when one hue is surrounded by another. Put two neighbouring hues together and each one will take on something of the other one's complementary component. For example, when orange is next to red the red will appear more violet, ie purple, and the orange will look more yellow.

Put a pair of diametrically opposite hues together and you will find that each appears more brilliant than when on its own. Opposite pairs are complementary; that is to say, they are one another's perfect contrast. I demonstrate this to myself by staring fixedly at my green plastic watering can. When I shut my eyes I can see a perfect image of it, except that it is red. This is *successive contrast*, a different thing from *simultaneous contrast*. The former involves an interval of time, while in the latter, each of two adjacent hues appears to be imbued with the after-image of the other.

Colours, therefore, change when they are next to other colours. You might fancy *Helianthus* 'Loddon Gold' no end and think it a lovely, soft, rich yellow when you see it in someone else's garden, but find it not nearly as genteel when it is in yours. What you may well have done is to plant it among blue cam-

panulas, which are driving it towards orange and giving it a tarty brassiness that sets your teeth on edge.

Tints and Shades

I am reluctant once again to take up cudgels against the 'anything but pastels is tasteless' school, but it has to be said that harmonising tints and shades of hues is far easier than doing so with pure hues themselves. It is greatly helped by the capacity of some hues to lose themselves as black or white are added.

Whereas red always retains its essential redness, as when it shades or tints to pink, yellow becomes apricot with white and olive-green with black, while orange becomes brown when black is added. Blue stays blue with white (as in the sky) but quickly becomes muddy and then grey when black is present, finally becoming almost indistinguishable

A feast of hot colours. Dahlias, hemerocallis, cannas and others combining to create a sub-tropical, torrid scene in a cool country. The brightness of the flowers is prevented from becoming overpowering by the generous amount of green foliage that is present

from black. It is interesting that many of the most ardently sought-after plants have flowers showing these sorts of colours; you only have to think of *Viola* 'Irish Molly', bearded irises like 'Gay Trip' and 'Lady River', roses such as 'Just Joey' and 'Glenfiddich', and many of the day lilies.

It is hard to go wrong with tints and shades. Without bright hues they are safe and those with poor colour sense or no understanding of how colour works can manage to produce effects that are pleasant enough and usually perfectly innocuous. But where is the fun, the excitement, the deep satisfaction that using strong colours brings to our inner selves?

The difference is the same as that between prettiness and beauty. Pastels are pretty; hues make for beauty. Who is followed by every eye – the English

Let pastels be lent impact by contrasting hues. Wake them up! Be adventurous. . .

Rose in her pink ball gown or the Latin in flaming red? Oh, of course, pastel shades and tints are eminently desirable, but let them be lent impact by contrasting hues. Wake them up! Be adventurous, but use a bit of thought at the same time.

If you have a bed in which there is a predominance of tints and shades from dark pinks, through lavender, lilac, mauves, violets and blues, throw in a bold dash of pure yellow and see what happens. The whole planting will come to joyous life, saved from dullness in one fell swoop. Why? Because yellow is the perfect complement to violet, on either side of which in the colour wheel are the darker reds and the blues.

Introducing Tone

Colour theory is really quite simple, yet its language is not. 'Hue', 'tint' and 'shade' are words with precise meanings but are made less easy because we use them as synonyms in ordinary speech. Up to this point, for the sake of simplicity, yet another such word, *tone*, has been left out.

Tone is a measure of the lightness and darkness of a colour. Light and dark tones are also referred to as high and low *values*. Tones include tints and shades, but also the luminosities of the individual hues.

Thus, yellow is the lightest in tone of the hues; violet is the darkest. As you follow the colour wheel from yellow to violet, each hue, or specific point on the wheel, is darker, or of lower tonal value than the last. From violet round to yellow again, the reverse obtains.

Tonal order is preserved in combinations of colours when a light tone of a light-toned colour is used with a dark tone of a dark-toned colour. For example, a light yellow should go with a dark red, but not a deep yellow with a light red. Similarly, a light orange will work with pink, whereas a deep orange will overpower it. Use pale orange with deep blue, but not dark orange with light blue. Don't forget that tones include tints and shades.

Assertive and Recessive Colours

Warm colours, which are hues in the yellow-orange-red part of the spectrum, tend to stand out and appear closer to the observer, especially reds. Cool colours – blues, greys, blue-greens and violets seem to recede. The colours may be termed assertive and recessive. It is most important to note, however, that white, that most cool of colours, is highly assertive.

Gertrude Jekyll, as we have seen earlier, made use of these qualities in designing borders so that they appeared longer than they, in fact, were. With the recessive colours at the ends and the assertive ones in the middle, the symphonic crescendos of her compositions had their roots in her sound grounding in colour theory. The theory, too, made her perfectly fearless in her use of the strongest, brightest and boldest colours.

Assertive colours may assert themselves so much that they can become detached and seem to float in space. That uncompromisingly naughty red dahlia, 'Bishop of Llandaff' (yes, him again) was used some years ago in an astonishing planting at Tatton Park, Cheshire. Its leaves are red-bronze and it was backed by *Berberis thunbergii atropurpurea*, whose foliage is nearly the same colour. In front was an edging of the almost-white foliage of *Senecio cineraria* (*Cineraria maritima*). The pure red flowers seemed to float without visible means of support, their stems lost against the background of the same colour. Furthermore, it was difficult to make out which flowers were in front of which until you stood closely over them.

This is an illustration of how very strong, very

Strong, assertive colours have a dramatic intensity when occurring among those that are mainly recessive. To have restricted the border to pastels and greys would have rendered it ordinary, as opposed to the sumptuousness that has been achieved by the inclusion of striking reds

assertive colours need to be given frames of reference. The white foliage defined the front, but the rest, while spectacular, was a trick – an optical illusion. Points of reference – small ferns, anything green or grey, for instance, or even a strong play of light and cast shade – would have imposed' order and perspective among the disembodied blooms. A green background would have made a much more restful composition.

The lesson from this is that areas of similar colour value need to be given structure. If you set out to be brave and plant a Jekyll-esque border – a proper one, not a tepid thing of finishing-school sobriety – it will get out of hand if you try for a climax of clamorous red with no leavening elements. Break it up with green in the shape of ferns, spring-flowering shrubs, grasses, or the foliage that comes before a late-summer takeover bid by white hydrangeas, and it will remain assertive but not overwhelming.

This is where the foliage of sun-loving perennials comes in, and is why your annuals should not all be of the sort that provide cushions of unmitigated colour. The foliage provides the structure that allows vigorous deployment of colour. Those who cannot handle colour sense this, but slide into that same old canard about colour being a thing of the moment but foliage always being with us. They hurry, like turtles to an algal soup, for the safety of universally compatible green.

Theory into Practice with Annuals

A nodding acquaintance with colour theory should enable you to work out why certain colour combinations have always made you feel uneasy. You should be able to get rid of such prejudices as 'gold with purple is vulgar' (it is, but light gold with dark purple is delightful), and you will find yourself making daring, dashing statements with splashes of bright, raw hue that you never thought possible. Prettiness, unless you truly admire it for itself, will become transformed into beauty.

You will be aware and wary of the changes that come over juxtaposed colours. Your sensibilities will expand away from the garden and you will realise just why her crimson-mauve dress clashes so foully with your scarlet-orange one; if yours were light, reddish orange and hers dark mauve, there would be no problem. You will use colour to create space, and above all you will buy, beg or sow plants whose flowers will bring you a full, singing joy and not frumpy, censorious dullness.

It is probably among annuals that the most ill-advised colour combinations are perpetrated. There is less room for manoeuvre with annuals, which have a general tendency toward forming domes and billows of colour without much structure-giving foliage. These sorts most certainly have their place, especially in small, formally or semi-formally arranged beds, and are seen at their best when variety is deployed sparingly. A series of round beds, each with a standard pink fuchsia and concentric rings of a soft pink 'geranium' encircled by an outer ring of white alyssum was a particularly appealing arrangement that found its way into the notebook one summer's day.

There are several, however, that can perform roles few perennials are up to, some of which, once you have grown them, are among the plants that you would never wish to be without again. Nicotianas are a classic example. Modern strains have their flowers open all day, rather than just in the evening, and they are notably fragrant. Their colours have a uniquely neutral effect, even the dusky reds, and they are perfect for filling the gaps that the best-ordered gardens must have where growing shrubs are properly spaced.

Hardy annuals can be sown where they are to

Nicotianas, dahlias and penstemons in the famous red border at The Priory, Kemerton, on the edge of the English Cotswolds. The owners of this garden have played a significant part in the movement away from blandness in garden colour

grow, so will fill spaces near to the root runs of the shrubs – spaces where damage would be done by digging if perennials were grown. Of all the nicotianas, 'Lime Green' is the one that will go with anything. There is no colour with which it clashes, and I have used it for several years running as my universal gap-filler. It is a graceful plant, elegant as any well-bred perennial, some 60cm (2ft) tall or more and flowering for weeks and weeks. The best results are obtained from sowing in early spring in heat and pricking out into individual pots, in which case there are flowers from late spring to autumn, but you must take care when planting them that nothing else is disturbed.

In more formal plantings, not necessarily on anything greater than cottage scale, the shorter dusky reds can be cunningly planted among nerines for a wondrously dramatic effect in early autumn. The matt, almost velvety, dark crimson, set against the crystalline pink that looks lit from within, is a fine example of using correct tonal order to make a beautiful contrast from two colours that would clash if of equal or reversed value.

Because of their long season, lime green and white nicotianas can provide long-term neutral colour facilities that shorter-lived perennial flowers can only provide for part of the time.

At the other end of the scale, as it were, Eschscholtzias (Californian poppies) bring a range of colours that is only provided among perennials by *Papaver orientale*. Their hues are purer, too, and nothing can match them for orange and orange reds. They would flower all year round if the climate would allow it, but it is still commonplace to find them blooming away six weeks before the winter solstice. Their place at the apogee of the Jekyllian border should be assured, and their filigree, grey-green foliage should be treasured as much as that of any perennial.

Osteospermums are really perennials but are generally too tender to overwinter. They are, in effect, a third kind of annual, to be kept going – and very easily – by cuttings taken in early autumn. There are some fairly awful names among them, but take no notice of coinings such as 'Gweek Variegated' and 'Lilac Whirligig'. Someone has given the alternative and unfortunately invalid name 'Tauranga' (pronounced Tauronga) to 'Whirligig'. It would be lovely if it caught on.

You can plant osteospermums just about anywhere in sun and they will grace the spot. Their flowers are silken daisies of subtle colouring, often slaty blue on the reverse, and they have an insouciant poise that opens all doors to them. If you were to seek an exemplar of the intangible qualities of a first-class plant you need look no further than those osteospermums not of the 'Whirligig', spoon-petalled type.

Large-flowered penstemons are among this third type of annual. The smaller-flowered ones like 'Sour Grapes' and 'Garnet' are hardy perennials, flowering until cut down in autumn, but those with large blooms are tender. They have a foxglove-like impact on a summer garden and are exotically surprising when emerging from a cloud of fennel or rearing up majestically beside a path.

Cosmos, china asters, *Argemone*, pyrethrums, and many more are also among the annuals that fit in happily with herbaceous perennials and shrubs in mixed plantings. They have character enough to stand up to the company of other plants that have been selected for being outstanding in their own field, and they provide colours that are compatible with the most cunningly devised schemes. It would be pointless to draw your attention to any more individually; go and see what is done in the great public gardens, keep your eyes open as you drive (the nicotianas and nerines were in a tiny garden in an English country town and almost caused an incident), and above all think of annuals as plants in their own right.

COLOUR PROGRESSION
IN THE BORDER

A border can be planted with any sorts of plants. In fact, the more the merrier and a mixed border is more interesting all year round than one devoted entirely to perennials, annuals or shrubs. For the time being, however, let us stay with what the world calls 'border' plants while we see what they have to offer in our search for harmonious but adventurous colour effects.

Blues
Among the most recessive colours is blue. Blues are self-effacing and try to disappear into the distance. The darker they are and the more purple, the more

recessive they appear. On the other hand, the purer the blue, the more it goes with anything.

Blue delphiniums are structurally assertive but recessive in colour. The Pacific Hybrids, a mixed strain, tend to have a good deal of mauve or purple in the blue and should be planted with their recessive nature in mind. They are best placed towards the ends of the border, where they can join the other blues (or presage them, in the case of campanulas) in heightening the illusion of space.

The named varieties in pure tints of blue can be bought true to type, and it is their assertive structure that is their great asset. They can be planted in

The impact of a colour does not only depend on its hue and tone, but also on several variables. The structure of the plant concerned is one, but the quality and intensity of incident light is another

clumps of three or more at even intervals along the border, where they will impose an ordered regularity that may only happen in early summer. If the border has a carefree look about it for the rest of the season, so much the better for it to enjoy a change of style for a short while. Delphiniums in blues unsullied by red or violet, such as 'Loch Leven' and 'Cristella', become very positive indeed when planted in this way – so much so that a pure white, such as 'Moonbeam', can take a turn in the order without taking any of the impressiveness from the blues.

The impact of a colour does not only depend on its hue and tone, but also on several variables. The structure of the plant concerned is one, but the quality and intensity of incident light is another. Colour is a function of the light it reflects or absorbs, and light is infinitely variable. Blue, above all others, is affected most by incident light.

The spring gentian, *Gentiana verna*, is one of the great joys of the European alps, studding the short turf not long after snow melt with a blue that is breathtaking in its purity. Take a photograph of it using an unbiased film such as Fujicolor and you will reproduce the colour, even without an ultraviolet filter. Now grow the gentian in a lowland

Incident light, south-western Britain: the sunlight of a summer's late evening

Incident light, south-western Britain: light overcast at mid-day in high summer

garden and see what happens. To someone who has not seen it in the wild it will appear the very essence of blueness, but to those who have there is a lack of dazzle, a toning down, a slight, almost undetectable hint of green. Take an unfiltered photograph of it and you will get, especially on a cool day, a slight, greenish overlay. You will never quite obtain the blue that your alpine picture gave you. The light at 2000m (6500ft) or more is a greatly different proposition from that at sea level.

It is not just elevation. Painters have for generations gone to St Ives, Cornwall, for the clear Atlantic light, where colours behave differently. My home in the south-west corner of Ireland, close to the Atlantic but with no industrial pollution for three thousand miles upwind, a high rainfall that cleanses the air of dust, and on an island with the greater part of its five million people crowded on the other side, has light of a diamond brightness that is beyond compare. All flower colours are intensified to an extent unimaginable to someone who has to live with the dusty, fumy air of a land where chimneys, cars and low-level ozone rule.

In the evening, your blue delphiniums will fade. Dark blues almost disappear in the crepuscular light; lighter ones become less vivid. White, on the other hand, becomes markedly more luminous. Your prefectural planting of delphiniums, blues with regular punctuation by white, will change dramatically as the sun goes down.

Blue has a great influence on white, purifying it and increasing its luminosity. Where you plant something white as an assertive note, the recessive blue will make it stand out even more. Perhaps the greatest variable of all in determining a colour's impact is its neighbours, and this factor, along with all the others, needs to be kept in mind whenever anything categorical is said about a colour.

Best Blues

Among the most well-loved blue border plants are the campanulas. Canterbury bells (*Campanula medium*) are biennials, often grown in blue and white mixtures with lupins, honesty and so on in a cottage-garden, tumbly mixture. The blue ones are beguiling at the far reaches of a border, looking almost as if they arrived by accident. Other campanulas are much more permanent, such as *C. persicifolia*, the peach-leaved bellflower, which comes in many shades (let us now revert to our usual usage of the word) of blue. Among the best is the clear powder blue of the semi-double flowers of *C. p.* 'Pride of Exmouth'. This is the only colour except white that you should accept in the nettle-leaved bellflower, *C. trachelium*. Again it is a semi-double form that you want; it is called *C. t.* 'Bernice'.

Campanulas are, as a whole, long-flowering, with most of the good ones staying in flower throughout the summer. Right at the end of the border is the place for *Campanula* 'Burghaltii', an unusual hybrid with large, dangling bells of soft blue-grey like the smoke from the tip of an idling cigarette.

Grey is chiefly an effect of foliage. Blue will make

grey appear cleaner, and grey makes true blues more intense. With grey-leaved plants you sometimes have to put up with flower colour that is assertive, but usually the blooms are so small that it does not detract from the coolness of your distance planting. Verbascums such as the biennial *Verbascum olympicum* have yellow flowers but they are often small and usually of a greyed yellow that fits in perfectly well. Try floating the round, grey-blue heads of *Echinops ritro* over the filigree of *Artemisia* 'Powys Castle' – this faultless, shrubby plant is hardy and hardly ever has any flowers at all.

Hostas with grey or blue-grey leaves, such as *Hosta sieboldiana*, fit in perfectly with the misty ambience of the border's end. It is so much the better if they have lilac flowers rather than white; in this particular species they are white, but with a lilac flush that quietens them down and keeps them in a back seat. Among the newer hybrids of this persuasion are 'Big Daddy', 'Blue Moon', 'Frances Williams', 'Wide Brim', 'Hadspen Blue', 'Blue Wedgwood' and, though I hate to admit it, 'Blue Umbrellas'.

Blues grade gently into mauves and purples as violet and red creep in. This is the colour range you see most among plants. There are many mediocre, wishy-washy colours between blue and pink and it is worth spending time over choosing those that

The long-lasting, globular heads of the 1.2m (4ft) globe thistle, *Echinops ritro*

have something more to offer than the tired mauve of great-grandma's afternoon-tea dress.

Day lilies are a temptation, but do try to choose vibrant colours from among the purples. *Hemerocallis* 'Chicago Royal Robe' is outstanding; a positive, rich colour such as Augustus might have ordered for the borders of his number one toga. As you move towards the dark reds, look for the deep ruby of 'Mallard' and the velvet textures of 'Gay Nineties' and 'Buzz Bomb'. Buzz Bomb? Whatever next . . .

Form often overcomes mediocrity of colour. If you were to find the pinkish mauve of acanthus flowers in, say, an aster, you might well dismiss it as anaemic. When it is part of the eccentric, bracted display put on by *Acanthus spinosus*, and to a lesser extent *A. mollis*, there is every justification for its inclusion.

Watch out for these purple tones though. Some can be truly excruciating and your hunt for positive, unmuddy colours may lead you to some of the more blatant realms of kitsch. This word does not just mean bad taste, a phenomenon which we may, by now, have come to agree upon as subjective, but either downright intolerable or so appallingly bad that it makes you laugh. Some of the hardy salvias are like that, with upright spikes of perfectly dreadful variations on magenta, redolent of mid-century Odeon or the interval bar of a cheap vaudeville joint. Choose *Salvia nemorosa* 'May Night' (which flowers on into September) and you could not wish for a more dramatic, clean, violet-purple.

As night falls, the rose 'Rambling Rector' will become more luminous, while the delphiniums will virtually disappear. While you look at this picture, half-close your eyes

Yellow

That yellow note among the mauves, purples and violets can be provided by almost anything you like, but it is a good idea to provide for a succession. You may choose a yellow day lily, such as *Hemerocallis* 'Esther Walker' or, if your border is on the small side, the delicious little *H.* 'Golden Chimes'. If you have space, plant both, as the latter flowers on well after the former. But for late effect, *Crocosmia* 'Solfaterre' (sometimes spelt 'Solfatare') is very special. Its iris-like leaves are light bronze and its clear, bright yellow flowers, just tinged with apricot, of the sort that look relaxed and natural, are graced with every intangible excellence that plants are heir to. Unfortunately, you will need a mild climate in which to grow it in the open border. Elsewhere it will need the shelter of a warm wall, where it can glow against the green of climbers. You may be tempted, in such a situation, to put it near nerines. Resist. The colour values are wrong and the warmth is drained from the crocosmia by the nerines, which then look icy cold instead of coolly lit from within.

Yellow is a tricky colour. There are, in fact, many yellows, but three main groups emerge. There are acid, greenish yellows, clear, pure yellows, and those that take on progressively more orange. The first group are cool, restful and pleasant when associated with plenty of green. The second kind are versatile and look right in almost any setting, while the third group are definitely warm and can be brassy and vulgar or delicate and elegant.

Yellow is an excellent buffer between colours that might otherwise clash, but the colour values have to be right. Two reds and a yellow, all of about the same brightness, can look about as aesthetically sophisticated as a table laid up for a children's party. A soft, slightly acid yellow, laid between two different rich reds, works much better.

Clear yellows are hard to place wrongly. They go with almost anything, but the one thing you must not do is to plant yellow in excess or fail to balance it with, at the very least, a great deal of green. Too much yellow creates an unpleasant dazzle and makes you yearn for velvety, violet darkness. It is best used to create rhythm in a planting – a grace note here, an accent there, a definitive statement on occasion, but a thread running through the general composition.

Yellow is a far more subtle colour than it is given credit for. Although the flowers of *Rosa* 'Frühlingsgold' are of a lighter shade than those of *Euryops pectinatus* (in the foreground) their effect is warmer

If your border is to have a colour climax, there is no need to fear clear yellow. It is assertive but accommodating and you can set *Heliopsis* 'Summer Sun' against a scarlet lobelia or the bright vermilion, self-opinionated *Lychnis arkwrightii* without playing *agent provocateur* to a war. If you are operating more conservatively, try the soft, clear yellow of *Helenium* 'Butterpat' as a background for pink dianthus and then throw in a white one for good measure. It is not a vivid combination but a strong one, full of cottagey promise, fulfilled if the dianthus are clove-scented.

Orangey yellows are hard to define. Some, becoming apricot, are softly warm and quite easy to place. Others, such as most forms of *Heliopsis scabra*, are brassy to some eyes, warm to others. None of us sees colours quite as other people do and this is another variable that precludes pomposity on the subject and makes remarks about 'taste' seem hollow. I actually like brassy yellows on occasion (such as when found unexpectedly among large, richly green leaves), but am well aware that some of the most revered plantsmen/designers avoid them like the plague.

Assertive as white may be, yellow can suppress it and lend subtlety to its presence. It can also moderate the influence of white on other colours. Take, for example, a grouping of bearded irises, in which a rich lilac variety is planted for contrast next to a white. The contrast is rather stark and the overall effect is cold. However, if a light, powder yellow and a rich, egg-yolk yellow are found on opposite sides of the combination, several things happen.

Firstly, any patterning on the lilac flowers, such as darker streaking or blotching on the falls, is emphasised. Secondly, the white is apparently toned down and calmed, and thirdly each yellow enhances and reinforces the other. The overall impression is now one of warmth instead of cold, and of subtlety where before there was only naiveté.

Yellow probably owes its almost universal matching qualities to our primeval inner eye. It is so close to green as to be part of it, so that in the 'Donegal Tweed effect', as it applies to green, some yellow is present. It is the main colour of falling deciduous leaves, and ochreous yellows are among the neutral tones of the ancient savannah where we first learned to run. Nevertheless, it is so varied that it is hard to say when it becomes brown or orange and it is not surprising that it gives rise to a wide

Where yellow is concerned we do well to trust our own instincts. . . Look at all the people who swooned at Van Gogh, only to find they had been admiring colours that had changed so much as to be barely related to the originals

range of opinion. Where yellow is concerned we do well to trust our own instincts and not to be led by peer group acceptance. Look at all the people who swooned at Van Gogh, only to find they had been admiring colours that had changed so much as to be barely related to the originals.

Whites

Why the passion for white en masse? What can be the attraction of having to keep constant vigil over flowers that become disfigured after every rain and unsightly when not far past their best? Is it some desire to show that one has a gardener – rather as white lace was worn at the wrist to demonstrate that one had no need to work? Because you sure need a gardener to do the dead heading if your white garden is of any significant size. Perhaps it is symptomatic of a thirst for virtue, quenched by its mere symbols? It is certainly not the sort of deviation to be practised by people living in the air of an industrialised nation, where finely-divided

kerosene and gas oil settle in a film over the pristine petals and the very rain threatens to sully their complexions with vitriol – dilute, admittedly, but damaging nevertheless. White gardens are fashionable and these remarks therefore unsociable, but at least go and look at a white garden with an honestly critical eye before you embark on such an absolutist exercise in monochrome gardening.

There are so many whites. Grey-whites, blue-whites, whites with a faint blush, creamy whites, dead whites and lively whites, translucent and opaque whites,. whites with markings and, as Casimir Malevitch showed us, whites on whites. They affect one another, as do all colours, and a blue-white iris will look dirty against a creamy-white one, an arum lily's opaque purity will downgrade that of a translucent waterside iris, and a frilled, double white dianthus will make a single one look grey. Can you really make a white garden look like fresh laundry, or must it nearly always have the appearance of dirty washing? The answer is not simple but boils down (if the phrase may be forgiven) to whether you possess unusual talent for arranging and looking after white-flowered plants to the required extent. If you have, good luck. If you have not – forget it.

Do not, however, forget white in your general colour scheme, particularly in your border. It provides buffers between warring colours and a strong system of punctuation, particularly in mirror-image beds on either side of a path, when white accents provide, with yellow, the visual clues that make you realise what you are looking at.

Because of the vagaries of white, it must be chosen with care. It is best, too, if your white-flowered plants have long flowering seasons, unless you are managing things so that there is an occasional change of scene, as when your delphiniums, planted in a certain sequence, give way to hollyhocks in another and you allow the white delphinium accents to drop out entirely. For example, wanting to use *Phlox paniculata* in a particular area, you might choose the very fine 'White Admiral', as pure a colour and as good a plant as you could wish. It will flower in late summer, but will stop while the border is still colourful and needing its presence. You can plant near it, or in a complementary position, the magnificent, late-flowering 'Fujiyama', which will pick up the baton of snowy whiteness with hardly a difference in quality.

Pinks

Pink is a deluding word. What is pink? You will read or hear about 'pure' pink, but there are many pure pinks. We all know roughly what we are talking about when we mention pink, but it is very roughly. What we can agree on is that pinks are tints of red. However, that means that they can vary from whited orange-reds to lightened versions of very dark reds and may have strong casts of blue in them, as in *Phlox paniculata* 'Excelsior', which tends towards lilac. Reds, notorious for supposedly clashing, are extremely peaceful when compared with pink, a race divided against itself in internecine tribalism.

But pink is an honourable colour! Pink is the darling of the well-bred young person who has been taught about 'taste'. Pink is the soul of gentility – after all, it was permissible for feminine underwear before we ever heard of permissiveness. Pink is . . . the refuge of those for whom strong, pure colours are intimidating. Sadly for them, it is a snare and a delusion, a staked pit in which waits a ravening bear; all that is worst in garden colour, the mismatch that manages also to be boring.

When you look at a pink (the colour, not the flower), refuse to call it pink. Ask yourself instead to hyphenate it with its main component. Is it orange-pink (*Sphaeralcea fendleri*), purple-pink (*Filipendula purpurea*), mauve-pink (*Monarda didyma* 'Croftway Pink'), carmine-pink (*Phlox paniculata* 'Cherry Pink'), or apple-blossom-pink (*Paeonia* 'Sarah Bernhardt')? If it is the last, you may find yourself saying, 'Well, it's *pink* pink', and so it is. You have, by elimination, discovered true pink, which is a tint of pure red.

This discrimination permits accuracy in placing pink flowers so that the mauvish ones, which are the most recessive, are allowed to warm up the near reaches of the mauve/blue/grey region of the planting, and redder and more orange pinks are released to take their more assertive place and cool down the more headstrong among the bright colours.

Reds

Red really does mean red – not pink. You can tempt two different reds to clash and get away with it to a certain extent, but let in a pink of a contrary persuasion and you can scrap the whole group.

Reds are hot colours, but vary in their heat. Blue-reds are relatively cold, orange-reds warm. The two do not mix well, but can be brought closer together than you might think in the presence of plenty of green. Tonal order is very important in managing reds; a light-toned orange-red will get along with a deep-toned blue-red, but not vice versa. Bright scarlet will go wonderfully with bronze-purple foliage, but blued-crimson much less so.

Red existed in our Old Adam world to attract our attention and that of pollinating insects, whether it was toward fruits or flowers. Nature rarely spreads red around in great sheets; it took man to create fields of poppies. Red does not need to be overdone to bring its full impact to bear. On the other hand, inharmonious distractions can ruin its effect altogether.

For a garden with space, where adventure is afoot and red is to be celebrated in a big way, all the tricks can be brought out of the box. Dahlias of swashbuckling pure red, such as 'Doris Day' and our friend 'Bishop of Llandaff' (two very religious people in mephisthophelean garb) are the sort of thing, along with *Lobelia cardinalis* and the best red penstemons, such as 'Ruby', to form the unadulterated heart of a festival of red. Green foliage will provide structure, perspective, and the essential foil for the red, while purple foliage makes for deep, toning shadows that suggest heat and mystery.

A collection of Michaelmas daises demonstrating the inadequacy of the unqualified word 'pink'

The colours can shade away towards the crimsons, blue-reds and violets in one direction, and head towards yellow, via the scarlets and orange-reds and orange in the other. Away then, cooling all the while, to where the blues and greys shimmer into the quiet distance.

Red as an accent in isolation is highly versatile – not as much so as yellow, but telling when just right. Make sure you use a red that will not spit and yowl at nearby pinks, surround it with green or 'purple' foliage, and do not be afraid of letting it loose near clear yellow. If you just bung it in willy nilly the chances are that it will be an eyesore.

There is no way in the world that you need to look on the Jekyllian, crescendo border as the ideal or even as an exemplar if your feelings and preferences lead you towards other styles. It is only one of the many, many ways in which perennials and annuals can be used in gardens and is the one chosen to illustrate the principles that lie behind the deployment of colour.

Perennials and annuals depend for their positioning on several things other than colour. The relationships that they have one to another in form, foliage and character, their heights and, above all, their flowering seasons are major factors. The principles apply, however, to anywhere that colour occurs in the garden, which is practically everywhere, and also whenever it is present. We have concentrated on summer, the season for annuals and most perennials; spring, with its cooler, lower light, has other things to offer.

The beginnings of a progression from hot to cool are evident in this display of dahlias. As ever, vulgarity is avoided when vivid colours are cushioned by green

CHAPTER 5

BULBS

The business of a poet, said Imlac,
is to examine, not the individual
but the species; to remark general
properties and large appearances.
He does not number the streaks
of a tulip.

SAMUEL JOHNSON

Cyclamen repandum and wood anemones beneath trees in springtime. Neither is botanically a bulb (they are tuberous and rhizomatous respectively) but for garden purposes such fine distinctions are irrelevant

Bulbs and spring are inseparable. The garden year starts with bulbs, and the vast majority of the bulbs we grow are spring flowering. Even so, we tend to forget that, while the classic harbingers of spring are snowdrops and crocuses, others of the same kind bring the year to an end. The year is non-linear; bulbs flower throughout, but it is in spring that they come into their own. Later they suffer the competition of the grand parade of perennials.

The bulb season proper extends from late winter to late spring. A quarter of the year is dominated by bulbs, but gardeners, for the most part, fail to make the most of them. In Holland they understand gardening with bulbs. A visit to a Dutch suburb, just a wander round the immaculate drives and avenues, will teach you more about bulbs than a stack of books, though it hurts your honest author to admit it. It will probably also provide you with a list of howlers and things to avoid.

This book is not really about the styles of gardening that involve planting bulbs in formal arrangements – blocks, concentric circles, and such like. If, however, that is how you like to plant them, good for you. It is a bold, bright, happy way to garden in spring. It is also labour intensive, but you will not want to do it if you cannot handle that. If you can manage colour, your garden will be a showpiece – but that's the rub.

Hyacinths are difficult to plant at all without their looking as though they will about face any moment and march off in their ranks towards the nearest warm room

Massed daffodils carry with them all the snags involved in using large quantities of yellow – too much dazzle, too many different yellows, and so on. Tulips come in raw colours without the leavening of foliage and need subtle handling. Hyacinths are difficult to plant at all without their looking as though they will about face any moment and march off in their ranks towards the nearest warm room.

We – you and I – have set our sights on a different kind of gardening. Although we respect and admire other disciplines, our target is the harmonious garden in which plants are plants and there are no

Forms of *Narcissus bulbocodium*, the hooped-petticoat daffodil, naturalised in the famous alpine lawn at the Royal Horticultural Society's Garden at Wisley, Surrey, England

categories. Paradoxically, in order to see where we are going, we have had to reassemble the plants into shrubs, perennials and other categories, and now we must recognise 'bulbs'. However, we will see them as members of the overall plant community, to be integrated into it, not as the objects of a show event.

A visit to the Keukenhof, the wonderful showplace of the Dutch bulb industry, is something every gardener may justifiably hope to achieve; how each one profits from the experience is another matter altogether. Different bulbs demand different settings. You will not find the little hoop-petticoat daffodil (*Narcissus bulbocodium*) bedded out in formal array. It is too dainty and leafy for that. Neither will the Keukenhof display *Anemone blanda* in geometrical blocks. To go to the greatest bulb garden in the world and come away impressed only by the Darwin tulips and tall trumpet daffodils is to have missed the whole point.

Part of that point is the very integration that we are aiming for. Leave the bedded-out displays and you will find bulbs growing harmoniously with early perennials, as well as providing foils and complements for spring shrubs. Bulbs, you soon find, are a sort of floral cement that brings the spring display together. It is against that background that the geometrical bedding schemes are planned and from it, astonishingly, that they seem logically and properly to progress. The Keukenhof, considering that it is divided up among many different growers, is a masterpiece.

Few of us are lucky enough to have the Keukenhof's seventy acres, and even the most industrious among us is unlikely to manage the six to seven million bulbs that are planted there each year. We must bring away from it, as from any other demonstration garden, the principles and understanding that will help us to enjoy our modest plots to the full.

The first such principle is naturalness. The main obstacle to the natural planting of bulbs is the time lag between planting and flowering. Good bulb planting needs good forward planning, as you have nothing to show for six months or so afterwards but bare soil. Similarly, you must see in your mind's eye the effect you desire a whole year before it can come to fruition.

What most people do is to find, suddenly, that the garden centre is full of racks of bulbs, with mouth-watering posters on the walls showing what lovely flowers they have. 'Ah, yes', they say, 'It's time we had some bulbs,' and, depending on how much their Christmas is going to cost, they load up; a handful of these, a bag of those; oh yes, and some of those over there.

Back at home it rains for three weeks. The wife says, 'What about those bulbs in the garage? Are you *ever* going to plant them?' You trudge out on the first day you can get on the soil, your hands cold, nose naggingly dropletted, and think of little but getting the damn things in and yourself back to the football. Spring eventually arrives and the bulbs are just where you don't want them. You decide to move them when the leaves have died down. The trouble is, you don't mark them, so when the leaves have gone you can't find the bulbs . . . let us draw a veil.

If you want to be reasonably well organised, there is no alternative to keeping a garden notebook. Even then you will probably need to supplement it with labels that say things like 'Plant *Narcissus* 'Ice Wings' here'. Your notebook may well have reminded you to buy some bulbs of 'Ice

Wings', a pure white cyclamineus hybrid of just over a foot high that you saw growing on a visit to a public garden. The entry was made in the midspring, the label perhaps even a year later. Having bought the bulbs the following September, you will be sure that they will come up where you want them to, two whole years after you first thought of them.

NATURAL PLANTING

Bulbs do not occur in nature in neatly arranged blocks. They seed themselves haphazardly around on the chance that enough seeds are going to find congenial places to germinate so that the species may be kept going. Like all plants, they demonstrate nature's complete lack of concern with the individual and her obsessive care of the species to which it belongs.

In nature, bulbous plants tend to grow in drifts where the soil and conditions are patchily suitable, and fairly regularly dotted about where it is of even quality but on the poor side. Bulbs never encounter soils to which horse manure, compost or fertilisers have been added until they invade or are invited into lands interfered with by man. Thus any planting in the natural style must take account of the exigencies of the wild and, at least, try to appear as if it had happened by chance.

This requires the use of the imagination. It also requires artistic flair, but one may venture to say

You may have a wonderful way with colour and a fine touch with design, but if you cannot think like a plant you will not get it quite right with bulbs

that the former is more important. You may have a wonderful way with colour and a fine touch with design, but if you cannot think like a plant you will not get it quite right with bulbs. The best gardening advice I was ever given was, 'Think like a plant'. It means, simply, put yourself in the mind of nature, imagine how she operates, and then try to emulate her. It helps with everything from planting an alpine in a crevice to breaking up the subsoil so that a tree's anchorage roots can penetrate it. In the case of bulbs it makes the difference between integrating bulbs and failing to.

To plant a small drift of bulbs, take a double handful and throw them away from you. Make very few adjustments, perhaps moving one or two away from a group that have fallen too close together, but always resisting the temptation to impose order. If the odd one goes too far, leave it. It will appear as just the sort of outlier that results when seed is blown across a patch of ground. Plant the bulbs where they lie.

Suppose now that you want to plant some daffodils beside the path that runs along side the lawn. The worst thing you can do is painstakingly to put them in at regular intervals in a strip along the edge. A lawn is not a natural place, but you can make it look a little more like an alpine pasture. Putting the imagination in gear, work out where the feet go as your herd (wife/husband and kids) turn in from the village road (emerge from the back door) and fan out, bells clanking, onto the mountain side

(lawn). Do they go near the path? Of course not!

There will be a narrow strip, shaped like a rounded lozenge, which receives less foot traffic than anywhere else. Plant your bulbs here, once again throwing them away from you and planting them where they land, but using just a little more artifice in arranging for outliers and tucking in any that wander into the area of heavy traffic.

Make sure you do not make the mistake of working this all out and then planting your bulbs alongside the terrace or patio. If you do, you will find that you were right about the winter traffic, but that in summer there are far too many feet. This is important because you must leave the foliage alone until it has fed the bulbs for the next year.

Bulbs (2): Natural planting by a lawn

A Area of minimum foot traffic
B Area of frequent summer traffic

C Area of maximum foot traffic
X Bulbs

Bulbs (1): Natural planting in a drift of *Narcissus* 'Ice Follies'

1 *Betula utilis*
2 *Acer palmatum*
3 *Azalea* 'Kure-no-yuki'

4 *Helleborus orientalis*
5 *Berberis thunbergii atropurpurea*

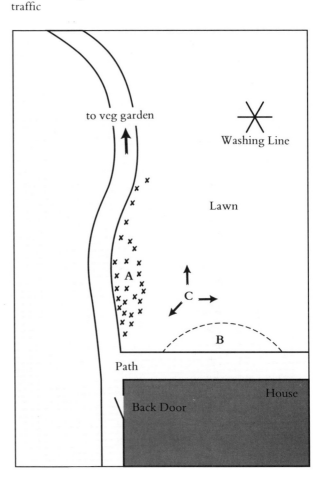

Bulbs in Context

Exhaustive studies carried out at Wisley, England, resulted in a report that said that the grass in which bulbs are growing should not be mown until six weeks have passed since the last flowers faded. My experience tells me that seven weeks is safer and eight even better. This means that if you plant bulbs that flower in mid-spring, such as many triandrus narcissi, jonquils and *Fritillaria meleagris*, it will be

The types of conditions liked by particular bulbs are, of course, all-important to their placing. As with so many kinds of plants, their very appearance often tells you where they want to be

approaching midsummer's day before you can safely mow. With some others it will be even later. This is no problem if you dedicate a little-used area to bulbs and mow neatly up to it, making a nice curved line, and if you have used your imagination and made it the least significant part of the lawn as far as practical and leisure pursuits are concerned.

Natural planting of this sort looks just right when the bulbs themselves look natural. What fits one

Tulips from Amsterdam – well, almost. The intrinsic formality of tulips, seen on a Dutch nursery in May

setting will not fit another. In a large garden you can drift-plant *Narcissus* 'King Alfred', a large, old variety you can buy in big sacks for not very much, or ring the changes with the white *N.* 'Mount Hood'. On a smaller scale you may come right down to *N. bulbocodium conspicuus*, only 12cm (5in) tall and like a busy crowd of tiny, gossiping ladies in yellow crinolines. By the same token, such a little treasure might look silly with photinias and hollies towering over it, while a minor change-up to *N. poeticus recurvus*, the 45cm (18in) pheasant's eye, would work very well.

The highly bred tulips do not lend themselves to these kinds of treatments. They are artificial creations, the work of three centuries of breeding, and no amount of cunning can make them look as if they dropped in by sheer luck. Where they succeed is in lawn-side beds where the setting is on the formal side. It may change as it gets further from the lawn, becoming woodsy and informal, but as long as there is a geometrical reference point near at hand – the lawn edge, a neat hedge, a hard path or a building, tulips in clumps or even in twos and threes will be in keeping.

The types of conditions liked by particular bulbs

are, of course, all-important to their placing. As with so many kinds of plants their very appearance often tells you where they want to be. Snowdrops, for instance, like nestling among shrubs or in the glades between trees, where they can settle down to long lives of building up wide colonies. Alliums enjoy flaunting themselves and their hot colours in full sun and associated with other exotica. Daffodils and narcissi just do not look as though they appreciate much of a baking in summer. To be on the safe side, however, it is best to familiarise yourself with

Some plants are just right as associates for bulbs; others are not, and in this respect your flair comes into play, as there is not much else to go on

their individual requirements before you plant them, and that means more research and yet another aspect to planning. Put *Allium* 'Purple Sensation' in woodland or *Anemone appenina* in a sunny scree and you will be lucky to see them flower once.

Bulbs in the wild associate naturally with other plants. While it is true that many do best where there is little competition, others are capable of wresting a living where there are shrubby or herbaceous rivals. Bulbs will often be found colonising ground where deeper rooted plants cannot survive; shallower soils, perhaps, where their bulbs soak up the summer heat that would kill plants that had not learned to become dormant. On the other hand, you will find bulbs that enjoy company and do not need a summer baking.

The safest compromise is to give bulbs areas of their own, if only for the practical reason that you will not want to disturb the roots of nearby plants in full growth when you lift dormant bulbs for propagation or just to move them. At the same time, try to plant them in a neighbourly fashion, so that they relate to the nearby plants, contrasting, complementing, reinforcing their messages or having their own reinforced. Some plants are just right as associates for bulbs; others are not, and in this respect your flair comes into play, as there is not much else to go on.

Because bulbs are individual plants of no great size (they become bulkier only by building up the number of individuals in a clump), you can make the relationships with neighbouring plants more intimate by slipping a couple of outliers into their root areas. For example, *Narcissus* 'Tête à tête', one of the very best and most scrumptious of the small daffodils, looks delightful in association with *Helleborus orientalis*, especially when the hellebore is present in its dark purple forms. The match works partly because the yellow of the narcissus and the dark tones of the hellebores are in the right tonal order, but also because it just works. The little daffodil has an unusually long flowering period and so do the hellebores, so they always catch one another for a couple of weeks' chat.

To mix them together at all thoroughly would be to create a messy mish-mash in which neither would gain. Each should be given room for expansion and the daffodil absolutely must be planted in bold patches and left for years to thicken up. It has two flowers to a stem – hence its name – and it is a shame not to make the most of its floriferousness. What you can do to enhance the relationship is to use one or two bulbs as seasonal fliers, planting them closely among the hellebores and lifting them after a year or two before they begin to look like more than chance, cheeky seedlings.

BULBS AS ACCENTS

There are many effects that can be created in bulb planting, but they boil down to two main kinds. On the one hand are the massed, meadow or woodland plantings such as a wide lawn, thickly bedecked with tiny daffodils, or a carpet of bluebells shimmering in the sunbeams. On the other, bulbs act as floral exclamation marks, prompting and punctuating the spring garden and drawing attention to neighbouring phenomena rather like bright schoolboys . . . 'Sir, Sir! Jones knows the answer!'

Classically, bulbs draw the eye to the bark and patterning of the trunks of trees. You might overlook the snakeskin bark of *Acer grosseri hersii* on a late-winter day as you hurry past, intent on cutting a cabbage before you freeze solid, but the first *Iris reticulata*, bravely – you might say rashly – thrusting their dark blue up through the perishing snow round its base, send out a vigorous message. 'Look

Cyclamen repandum. In planting this colony, a shaded, out-of-the-way patch of soil has been converted from somewhere to be ignored into an intriguing feature that turns one's feet from the nearby path

at us! Look at us! We're here, you know!' How can you fail to stop and notice the sweetly patterned trunk with its small, optimistic, blue acolytes?

The intricate twistings of the roots of an old tree, spreading and splayed on the ground like sleeping snakes, are not something that you would look at normally with any sense of wonder. Plant winter-flowering cyclamen (*C. coum*) among them, however, and the little red, pink or white flowers and dark green leaves tell many a tale of being snugly contained and cared for by the reliable old roots, to whose sinuous presence they draw your otherwise unheeding attention.

Perhaps we should define our terms. By 'bulbs' we loosely mean plants with storage organs that are bulbs, corms or tubers. Loosely, because some with such roots (*Geranium tuberosum*, corydalis, dahlias, for example) fall into the realm of perennials; so much for categorisation. The winter aconite, *Eranthis hyemalis*, has a tuberous root and is sold by bulb growers, although it is strictly an herbaceous perennial. I do not think it matters one whit when it glistens like blobs of molten gold beneath trees at the end of winter, brightening the shade and providing the perfect company for snowdrops.

The role of bulbs as exclamation marks goes a long way towards providing atmosphere. This is particularly so in spring, when they are a major factor in the floral scene. In summer they tend to be an adjunct to the display put on by annuals and perennials. Spring colours are generally soft – a good thing, as the light is soft and untropical – but bulb colours vary from the gentle to the positively raucous. This means on the one hand that you have to take care in their use, but on the other that they can bring excitement and dash into the garden.

When we were looking, in the last chapter, at the variables that influence colour and our appreciation of it, the influence of light was mentioned, but not that of seasonal light. Now, with a mental picture of tulips in spring, we can think about it to some effect. Summer light, hot and brilliant (we hope), demands stronger colours than the shallowly slanting light of spring that is so much more diffused by its long passage through the atmosphere. Thus, you welcome the blue of scillas, chionodoxas and European bluebells and, like Perdita in *The Winter's Tale*, '. . . daffodils, that come before the swallow dares, and take the winds of March with beauty'. Isaac Watts recognised the link between bright colours and the onset of summer:

> *The tulip and the butterfly*
> *Appear in gayer coats than I.*

Yes, but the tulip is a spring flower. How do you reconcile the flaming orange-scarlet of *Tulipa praestans* 'Fusilier' and the brilliant scarlets, oranges and aggressive yellows of tall hybrid tulips with the toned-down palette of spring?

One answer is that you do not. Well, at least you do not appear to. You return to the colour theory that stood you so well when planning the planting of perennials and construct contrasting accents that herald summer and its harder light. Mid-season daffodils of lightly toned, creamy yellows ('Carlton' is too richly yellow, but 'Daydream' is just right) can be accented by clumps of tulips such as 'First Lady' *but not too closely at hand*. The styles of flower are not sufficiently compatible for apposition, but with the reddish violet-purples of the tulips against and among green, but seen in the same glance as the daffodils, the point is made.

Bright reds against green never offended anyone, and they certainly do not upset the notion of spring. As long as the brighter, harder colours do not come into direct conflict with the softer tones, your spring picture will retain its integrity. This concern is not a matter of tonal order but of strength tending to overcome gentleness.

However, you can integrate the brightest red tulips into the spring palette by planting them away from other bulbs and matching them to the newly emerged leaves of *Pieris* 'Forest Flame' or 'Bert Chandler', whose pinks and reds owe nothing to modesty. If you do not have the required acid soil, make the match with *Photinia* × *fraseri* 'Red Robin'. Its newly unfurled leaves are worthy rivals to those of the pieris and are not as likely to be nipped by frost, as well as lasting for months, rather than weeks.

A YEAR OF BULBS

Whether they are tiny crocuses, peeping up at the spring sun and hoping it is here to stay, or stately lilies, coolly perfumed on a sultry July day, bulbs are plants of immense character and presence. Analyse this and you will find yourself with little more to consider than flowers and colour; perennials have far more to offer as far as foliage is concerned and bulbs cannot begin to compare with woody plants for diversity of interest. It must be the intangible characteristics of bulbs that lend them that portion of their impact not derived from their colours, but to attempt to describe them is only to turn such terms as elegance, stateliness and so on into worn-out discards.

One way of beginning to understand what it is

For those (such as the author) who find lilies difficult, *Lilium longiflorum* is the answer to their prayer. It is remarkable for the speed with which it reaches flowering size from seed, and the F$_1$ Hybrid 'Snow Trumpet', sown indoors in early spring, will flower within five months. That it is not easy to keep from year to year hardly matters when you can guarantee flowers 15cm (6in) long with a heady, carrying fragrance

about bulbs that is so captivating is to break into the year's cycle at some point and follow it round to that point again, seeing what a year of bulbs can do for the garden. The most logical point to choose is January in the northern hemisphere; July in the southern. For clarity, let us call it mid-winter, with the following month being late winter, the next one (March/September) early spring, and so on.

Snowdrops

The snowdrop season starts in the mid-winter month. There are many species of snowdrops, but most are the province of collectors. However, far too many gardeners think that there is only one – *Galanthus nivalis*. The earliest snowdrop robust enough to endure through thick and thin is *G. byzantinus*. It varies in height, but the taller forms are noble little plants with large flowers. Snowdrop flowers are composed of short inner and long outer segments and their white is often marked with green. In this species the green blotches are at the bases of the inner segments. *G. nivalis* starts late in the month, spreading its white, nodding bells with just the tips of their inner segments marked with green among the fallen leaves of last autumn, thrusting up through frost-rimed ground without a care for the chills of winter.

Snowdrops are curiously ineffective when growing on bare soil. When their pearly flowers are seen against grass, even when it is strewn with the debris of a dozen winter gales, they have a freshness and an air of saluting the turn of the year that is absent when their leaves lie like muddy, green starfish on rain-splashed soil. This is the secret of their charm; they naturally like to live undisturbed, building up colonies by seed and multiplication of the bulbs where there are woodland glades affording minimal competition from larger plants. They have evolved to have the maximum attention-drawing capacity when part of a sward and are not creatures of barren brownness.

Grassy places among shrubs, or specially chosen, small areas where the lawn runs up to trees or tall shrubs and is shaded and can be cut late, will allow snowdrops to broadcast to the full their cheerful optimism for the slowly lengthening days.

Cyclamen

Cyclamen coum appears during the mid-winter month, but may come before or after it, depending on variety, as it is a conglomerate species, the plaything of taxonomists. For such a small plant it has maximum impact, but depends for it on being quite un-spring-like in its colouring. The flowers, like miniature ship's propellers, are strongly crimson, magenta, or in a range of pinks that are all on the purplish side, but never remotely mauve. White ones serve only to make the point more forcefully.

The presence of cyclamen is often felt most strongly when they are a surprise, occurring suddenly round a corner under an otherwise temporarily forgotten shrub. *Cyclamen coum* is a surprise all in itself, however, and its hot little flowers leap out at you from amid their frigid surroundings and the leaves, anything from round and plain dark green to cordate and beautifully marbled, are seductively deep crimson on their lower sides.

Snowdrops, *Galanthus nivalis*, contrast with *Crocus tommasinianus* in both colour and form

Plant it in colonies beneath *Hamamelis mollis* and see if you can stay indoors for long when cool, yellow, spidery, scented flowers wreathe the bare branches above the summery tones of the cyclamen, woven into a carpet worthy of Tabriz or Isfahan.

Iris

The mid-winter month sees the start of a little flurry in iris activity. *Iris histrioides* is the earlier of two reliable species that do not, as others do, flower once and then break up into masses of wheat-like bulbils that take several years to gather the strength for another bout. It is only 4 cm (1½in) high, but the flowers are as wide as that and bright royal blue. The falls are marked in white and gold and the flower stands up to any amount of rain and even frost when fully open. *I. reticulata* is the one everyone knows. It is a little taller and more slender. The reddish-purplish-mauve-blues are the most usual colour forms, but they are not nearly as effective as the light blues – 'Cantab' and *I. r. cyanea* – and the deep sky-blues, 'Harmony' and 'Joyce'.

These blue irises, which often flower through the snow, are powerfully cheering just when you thought winter was going to go on for ever. It still may, but life without illusions is much less fun.

Crocus

Crocuses have two main seasons; late winter/spring and autumn. There are so many of them that only a few are readily recognised by most gardeners, but it is worth getting to know a few more. The large 'Dutch' crocus come later in the spring and are best in broader situations than the average garden, into which they fit uneasily. Drifts among orchard trees look wonderful, and such a place, where the grass can be left unmown until the middle of summer, is best for them.

The others in the early group take us from the quiet of winter to the busyness of mainstream spring. *Crocus laevigatus* and *C. l. fontanayi* lead off even before the snowdrops, with the happily spreading, but never naughty *C. tommasinianus* following with its slender, lilac-mauve flowers cropping up everywhere once it takes to you. It is a benevolent coloniser, endearingly enthusiastic, to be given its head as long as it promises not to mind if you ignore it and dig it about when looking after other plants.

The late winter month sees the burgeoning of *Crocus chrysanthus*. You will not often see the species; it is so variable that it has given rise to colour forms from deep, egg-yolk yellow to smoky grey-blue. Its forte is in brightening chirpily the more intimate places of the garden – tubs, urns, raised beds, the rock garden – and in making you want to draw close to see the deep brown veining on the yellow 'Zwanenburg Bronze', the rich orange stigmas in the pale blue 'Blue Pearl' or the dark lilac feathering on the white of 'Snow Bunting'.

Anemones

As crocuses dot the sunnier, open parts of the garden, colourful against the gradually freshening green like a game of 'Go' played with fairy snooker

The intense sapphire of *Anemone blanda* belongs in sun, reflecting the sharp light from its luminous petals

balls, anemones appear, cool and *soigné*, on what on an American golf course would be called the first cut of rough. They like to be able to anticipate shade. The sky-blue *Anemone appenina* and the faintly blushed *A. nemorosa* are truly spring flowers, full of the daintiness that proclaims the staying of the clumsy, chapped hand of winter. *A. blanda* belongs in sun and shows it. Its colours, sapphire, white and near-ruby, strike almost a false note and need careful handling, perhaps only in character in larger gardens on warm, open hillsides, where wide drifts in short turf can reflect a sharper light.

Daffodils and Narcissi

Of the so-called botanical narcissi, many are exquisitely beautiful but so early flowering and so liable to be battered by weather that they need protection. This in no way belies their loveliness nor their appeal for gardeners who enjoy growing bulbs in alpine houses and frames, but it means that their impact on the garden is minimal. Those that can stand up to outdoor conditions are the only ones with a role in the harmonious community of plants that we are seeking to create.

This does not rule out some of the most beautiful of all. As we have already mentioned, *Narcissus bulbocodium* is an unforgettable sight in an alpine-meadow setting transferred to the garden. Some forms are tender or too early, but two, *N. b. citrinus*

Narcissus 'February Gold' is in a class of its own for significance, but many others jostle for places among trees and shrubs where no hint of formality can spoil their air of leaning into a fresh breeze

and *N. b. conspicuus*, flower one after the other as spring begins to enter its middle phase, and are as hardy as you could wish. Their moment is all too short and their effect on the emotions is chiefly one of regret – regret that you have to wait another whole year before seeing their hooped petticoats again.

The cyclamineus hybrids, whose petals are to a greater or lesser extent swept back, cyclamen fashion, are among the most well loved of the small

narcissi that are not too far removed from species. *Narcissus* 'February Gold' is in a class of its own for significance, but many others jostle for places among trees or shrubs where no hint of formality can spoil their air of leaning into a fresh breeze.

'Botanical' narcissi and miniature daffodils are earlier, in the main, than the larger 'garden hybrids'. The same goes for 'botanical' tulips. To be honest I never know where I am with the terms used by the show fraternity; the difference between a daffodil and a narcissus has never engaged my attention much. However, I take botanical tulips to be those not far derived from species and having the characteristics of them, rather than of the highly bred Darwins, Triumphs, Parrots *et alia*.

Tulips

The species and 'botanical' colours can, if anything, be harder and brighter than those of their urbanised cousins. *T. linifolia* is brilliant scarlet with narrow leaves and is usually recommended for the rock garden. Fair enough, but it can be well out of kilter with the soft colours usually found there and is much better on its own in a hot, well drained place where its message can be belted out with the power and verve of a floral Edith Piaf.

The two most usually grown groups of botanical tulips are the greigii and kaufmanniana hybrids. Tulips as a whole are notoriously difficult to keep going from year to year, especially in cool, moist climates and heavy or moisture-retaining soils. You find yourself going to all the bother of marking and lifting them for storage or you shrug and buy afresh every year. Some people, who like their gardens to grow with them and to whom such operations are anathema, do neither and stop growing tulips. However, the tulips in these two groups are almost indestructible and will take all sorts of abuse in soils that are otherwise most inhospitable to the genus.

Greigii tulips are distinguished by their broad leaves, which are prominently marked and steaked with dark, brownish purple. The best known variety is *Tulipa greigii* 'Red Riding Hood', 20cm (8in) tall and bright scarlet. Kaufmannianas are the water-lily tulips, which are mostly a little shorter. *T. kaufmanniana* itself is creamy white with carmine bases to the petals, and the colours are generally not as fierce as in the greigii kinds.

Fosteriana tulips flower a week or two later than the 'botanicals' and are the basis of the Darwin

Hybrids, in which they are crossed with Darwins, now included in the new classification as Single Lates. You may well throw your hands up at all this stuff; we have already lost our floribunda and hybrid tea roses to the bureaucratically insipid Large- and Cluster-flowered designations. Now Mendel, Cottage and Breeder Tulips have gone and poor Darwin (not for the first time) is threatened. Will Rembrandt disappear eventually under the general term 'Broken'?

Fosterianas are an ideal group if you want a display of Darwin-type tulips in the smaller garden. One or two, such as the 50cm (20in) 'White Emperor' – incidentally the best and longest-lasting white tulip of all – are uncharacteristically tall, but the large-flowered, red 'Princeps', vermilion 'Cantata' and pure yellow 'Candela' are around half that height. In a city garden, where you may have to operate a bedding system of some sort or other in order to have any sort of a continuous display, a formal arrangement of fosteriana tulips can provide brilliant colour for a month in the middle of spring.

Mid-season Bulbs

The mid-season for the bulb world occurs towards the second half of spring and almost into summer, when bulbs seem to disappear from garden significance almost overnight. The large tulips and the narcissi broadly known as small cupped are the main features, and enough has been said about them. Their presence can be made even more forceful, however, by a little judicious use of other bulbs. A drift of white-and-yellow daffodils such as the tazetta 'Minnow' or the poeticus 'Actaea', both of which are deliciously scented, will be perfectly set off by a small, discreet, naturally-planted group of muscari, their blue enhancing the purity of the narcissi.

Muscari look out of place on rock gardens, which is where you so often see them. They are stiff little plants and need the languid grace of narcissi to give them a point of reference, otherwise they are as embarrassed in the same way as outdoor hyacinths; right dress, wrong dance.

Crown imperials – *Fritillaria imperialis* – are indeed plants with impact. Their stout, upright stems 80cm (32in) high, each thrusting its terminal whorl

Tulipa linifolia. This species tulip is 15cm (6in) high and flowers during the second half of spring

of red, orange or yellow flowers imperiously above lesser vegetation, would seem, at first thought, to be outlandish and hard to visualise in harmonious settings. Yet wherever they are planted they seem, particularly the lemon-yellow sort, to be just right, heaven knows why. You must plant a bold group

———— ❦ ————

*Crown imperials – **Fritillaria imperialis** – are indeed plants with impact. . . They defy all efforts at related planting, so do not even try*

———— ❦ ————

of them, though – preferably more than one – and let them do their thing at the sunny fringe of a group of shrubs. They defy all efforts at related planting, so do not even try. Crown imperials are summery in their appearance but flower in mid-spring, when they herald the turn from spring into summer among garden bulbs. You may hear that they often fail to flower, and so they do. The reason is that they are potash-hungry; dress in autumn with $33g/m^2$ ($1oz/yd^2$) of sulphate of potash and the problem should be solved.

The Crown Imperial, *Fritillaria imperialis*

Ornamental onions may not sound like the best thing since bakelite but they create effects as no other plants do, and they are visual effects, too, not olfactory. There are two main groups, those with round heads of flowers like tennis balls, and those whose flowers droop, either as a group or of individual stalks.

Of the first group, *Allium* 'Purple Sensation' is more than typical, it is one of the very best, with large heads of purple-rose. It can be planted fairly

Ornamental onions may not sound like the best thing since bakelite but they create effects as no other plants do. . . they are among the best plants we can grow: hardy, reliable, easy and beautiful

closely among perennials or set in a group, hot-country fashion, to stand proudly alone in a gravelly place with cool colours and foliage behind making an intriguing contrast. *A. christophii* has enormous, spherical flower heads, 25cm (10in) across, of that metallic blue-mauve only found elsewhere in callicarpas. It is not that tall – only 60cm (2ft) and makes a wonderful surprise when planted among early summer perennials that over-top it, irises for example. After the flowers are done, the seed heads hold their shape and turn brown, remaining ornamental for months. *A. cernuum* almost matches the colour of *A. christophii*, but is more inclined to pink. It is not as tall – about 45cm – but typifies the elegance of the drooping-flowered alliums and is at home anywhere among the shorter perennials of the border-front.

How often do you see these lovely exotics in gardens other than the public and botanical ones? Not often – and yet they are among the best plants we can grow; hardy, reliable, easy and beautiful. If they were called 'perennials' or 'herbaceous' they would be seen far more often, I am sure, but their place in the 'bulb' pigeon-hole puts them on the periphery, neither part of the Great Spring Bulb Show nor of the Summer Parade of Perennials. That they are 'onions' detracts from their market-ability. In fact, they are the stuff of an ad-man's nightmare; the product is excellent but the story is rubbish.

Summer Bulbs

Summer-flowering bulbs are not all that easy. Dahlias are usually sold by bulb merchants, but their role in the open garden is as perennials, to be left in place in mild climates and lifted for winter storage elsewhere. Gardeners are divided on the use of the dahlia; some see it as an exhibition flower, out of character in the open border, others throw it in among the rest of the plants with abandon, letting the bright yellows, rich oranges and can-can reds kick up their heels in the summer sun.

Good for them! You are just as likely to see flamboyant dahlias in the sort of border that lies below a series of terraces at the rear elevation of a great house (you know the sort of thing, it's the last feature before the ha-ha) as rioting in a cottage garden on the estate. The nobs up at the Big House probably swap them with the cottagers anyway; gardening is a great leveller when allowed to be.

Gladioli are in the lift-for-the-winter league. There are some small ones, the Nanus gladioli, that are less stiff and presumptuous than the Edna Everage gladdies that only look really at home wrapped in ribbon and tissue. You must, for once, forgive what is undoubtedly prejudice and allow a mere nod in the direction of the undoubted impact of gladioli. They are not everyone's cup of tea, possums.

The wonderfully tropical tigridias, large-flowered and sumptuous, are worth renewing annually, and so are cannas. Cannas are not bulbs at all, but fleshy-rooted perennials. So what! Their huge, paddle-shaped leaves, green and glossy or tinged richly with maroon-mahogany make the tropics seem just down the road when the strangely-shaped flowers in hot colours – orange, red and vivid yellow – emerge in late summer. They need to be lifted for winter, but who cares when they are such a magnificent feature and such a perfect foil for all sorts of earlier-flowering plants. So why mention them here? Because *Galtonia candicans*, tall of stem and a-dangle with cool, white bells, *is* a bulb and is never so lovely as when it lifts its limpid blooms against the wide blades and torrid tones of canna lilies. It is the ice in a tropical cocktail.

Cannas are not lilies at all. True lilies flower earlier in summer and are lovers of cool places. *Lilium candidum* is more fond of sun, always managing to adjust itself so that its nose is just out of the

Allium **'Purple Sensation', one of the aristocrats among bulbs, stands on its dignity with those with the effrontery to call it an onion**

ground. It is another plant that could do without being known either as a lily or as a bulb, as it is made for the border, where it associates perfectly with blue – really blue – delphiniums. It is not called the Madonna lily for nothing, and the blue serves to make its whiteness even more sweetly virginal than it is already.

There are many, many lilies, the majority of which are either way over the top as far as colour and decoration with spots goes, or very difficult to grow. Lilies like some gardens and gardeners, while they loathe others so much that they wish them-

selves to death in no time. You might gather that this is written by one whose success with lilies is minimal. It is a matter for sorrow when one's best efforts result in failure, year after year after year.

Lilium regale, however, possibly the best of all lilies, grows well even for me. It likes sun or part-shade and is not too fussy about soil. Grown in groups among low shrubs like Japanese azaleas, it gradually increases the number of tall stems (1.8m – 6ft – sometimes) it produces, on which are borne as many as thirty large, white, funnel-shaped flowers with blushes of deep pink on the outside. 'Royal Gold' is a cool, quiet yellow, and both forms are sweetly scented. They flower for a long time, start-

———— ❧ ————

Cyclamen hederifolium *is one of the wonders of cool-temperate gardening; hardy, indomitable, immensely long-lived, and as reliable as a station master's watch*

———— ❧ ————

ing in mid-summer, and if, like me, you can only grow one lily really well, take heart, as this species is a queen among plants.

Amaryllis belladonna is a summery plant, flowering in early autumn. Its enormous bulbs send up stout stems about 75cm (30in) tall, each of which bears two to four large, trumpet-shaped flowers. Typically they are pale pink, but selected forms, of which more are appearing as the species is more widely grown, are often more richly coloured. It is not a bulb for cold regions and needs summer heat. The best place for it is at the foot of a warm wall. Quite honestly I think *Crinum* × *powellii* is a better bet. It also dislikes cold places but does not need as much heat nor as many years before its flowers appear, and it is very similar to an amaryllis. It likes just the same conditions as agapanthus.

Agapanthus are members of the Liliaceae but are perennials, not bulbs. They are among the aristocrats of blue-flowered plants, but it is difficult to explain why; you must see them for yourself, if you are not already familiar with them. If they are described as having strap-shaped leaves and 90cm (3ft) stems bearing onion-like heads of flowers, some of which are upright and some of which are drooping, you will think them very dull. That description is, of course, to leave out the intangible qualities of agapanthus, which are considerable. The arching of the leaves, the way a clump gains dignity as it increases, and the separation of the

Crinum x *powellii*, whose large, soft pink flowers seem made for the gentle light of late summer evenings

flower stems so that each has its own impact but together they stand out as a major feature – all these have something to do with it. Be careful, though. Plant them too closely to a tall background and they will run for the sun, leaning outwards and sideways like passengers on a wall of death, and their whole effect will be ruined.

But we were talking about *Crinum × powellii*. Well, we still are, because one of the most wonderful late summer combinations of bulbs is to grow it in the company of blue agapanthus. The light pink and the rich blue are tonally perfect, and they come at a time when many gardeners are already thinking about autumn colour, bonfires, and ordering the turkey.

Agapanthus species are on the tender side, but trials of agapanthus held at Wisley in the 1970s surprised everyone by demonstrating that many, especially hybrids, were far hardier than had been thought. The race called Headbourne Hybrids, some of which have been given varietal names, are hardy almost anywhere. For a different kind of combination, try blue agapanthus, especially dark ones ('Lilliput' is about the darkest and neatest and the best for small gardens) alongside *Crocosmia* 'Solfaterre'. I tried them together after having read of it as a suggestion by Graham Stuart Thomas and was delighted with the result.

Cyclamen hederifolium is often called 'the' autumn-flowering cyclamen. In fact it flowers in late summer and just the beginning of autumn, and it is its leaves that give so much to the fall and winter. There used to be great, sweeping drifts of it under and near trees at the old Gavin Jones nursery at Letchworth, in the English Home Counties, and there it must have inspired thousands of gardeners. It is one of the wonders of cool-temperate gardening; hardy, indomitable, immensely long-lived, and as reliable as a station master's watch in the days of steam. Few flowers are so perfectly like jewels, strewn among short grass or studding well-mulched soil with pinks of varying richness, interspersed with white.

Autumn Bulbs

Autumn has its own crocuses. The crocus season really starts then and goes on until spring, a demonstration of the fact that the gardening year knows no beginning and end but those we create purely for the sake of the narrative. *Crocus speciosus*, typically lavender-mauve but approaching true

blue in some varieties, is the most valuable of them, sharing with *C. tomasinianus* of spring its toleration of being forked or dug over. *C. cancellatus*, a variable plant that can flower at any time in autumn, and *C. kotchyanus*, which is early, make up with it a triumvirate that puts autumn crocus among the most important bulbs. However, human nature being what it is, autumn is the neglected season in gardens and they do not get their fair share of the action.

Colchicums are universally called 'autumn crocuses', which just goes to show how neglected the real ones are. Like them, they flower before the leaves appear and stand bereft of foliage like footless goblets mischievously balanced on their stalks overnight by the little folk. The best species is

---

Bulbs go with everything and hold everything together. . . they should be released from the bondage of custom and set free to bring together all the elements of the harmonious garden

---

Colchicum speciosum, which flowers in autumn and not late summer, and there are many named colchicum hybrids, some of which are indistinguishable one from another but all of which are dramatic, attention-seeking bulbs.

A scatter of crocuses tiptoes over winter to link up with the spring acceleration of bulb flowering, and the year is done. There are many more bulbs, but the point is made. Why be so detailed in outlining the bulb year? Simply because bulbs are different. Rarely are they appropriate when seen on their own, unless in Keukenhof-style bedding. Even in that great garden they demand some kind of reference to other plants, and in our gardens they are what in medicine would be called 'universal donors'. Bulbs are like the lustre fibre in a weave that converts it from a matt cloth to a shimmering fabric, fit to clothe a great beauty. They go with everything and hold everything together. They are the ultimately isolated category of plants as far as the market and literature go, but of all categories they comprise the one that should be released from the bondage of custom and set free to bring together all the elements of the harmonious garden.

CHAPTER 6

SCENT, ROSES AND CLIMBING PLANTS

. . . any nose
May ravage with impunity a rose.

ROBERT BROWNING

The subtle, delicate scent of *Rosa banksiae* 'Lutea' lent a
light touch of early summer fragrance to the visual charm
of this conference of climbers at Chelsea, 1991.

In his *Philosophical Dictionary* of 1764, Voltaire reminds us that, while we are astonished at thought, sensation is equally wonderful. Perhaps, as gardeners, given to intellectual modesty and a love of nature, we might reverse his dictum; for we surely feel that thought is wonderful but are astonished by sensation.

Certainly scent has the power to astonish over and over again. We mentioned briefly in Chapter 1 the fleeting nature of scent, how it cannot be pinned down and subsequently cannot truly be remembered. When a scent is re-encountered, it floods our consciousness with associations and remembrances,

A scent is a scent, whatever kind of plant produces it, and the impact a scent has on us has much to do with how the plant originating it is positioned in the garden

often hitherto completely forgotten. Astonishment may well be the least of the emotions it engenders.

Flower scents are among the most powerful of all. Like all fragrances, they are highly subjective and personal. For me, frangipani means the banyan-shaded Whitehead Street in Key West and lemon blossom takes me to the Villa Vico Bello near Siena. Daphnes instantly replay a pause on the steps near the lily pool at Wisley, and the hot-caramel aroma of gorse is forever linked to summer walks by the river bank in Ireland.

Such connections lend an almost substantial quality to scent. One's mind builds up a network of references and labels for individual odours, so that similies abound and things begin to have scent only as a function of something else. 'Hot caramel' is one; 'pineapple' and 'greengage' are others, as we saw earlier. It can't be helped, because we need such touchstones in order to be able to discuss scent at all. What we should hold fast to, however, is the gentle tyranny of scent, its unexpected, momentary swamping of our sensing selves; its ability to wake up Old Adam and stand him right alongside his Modern Citizen counterpart. Both the acquired and the atavistic parts of us react equally; the response to an exquisitely fragrant flower and the perfume from a swirl of silk is in each case simply, 'Wow!'

The plantsman will react to scent and will count it among the virtues of a plant. The most famous of all living plantsmen, not greatly known for garden design (although a master planter) takes great pains to find a spot near his front door for plants with outstanding perfumes. Designers, on the other hand, seem curiously unwilling to commit themselves on the subject. You would think, would you not, that it would be the other way round?

A designer/plantsman (or plantsman/designer), which is what you have become if you have stayed thus far without skipping too many pages, will take as much notice of scent as of any of the other qualities of a plant, tangible or intangible. He (she) will count it of importance both at the choosing stage and during planting.

There are a great many plants with significant scents, falling into all the categories. Among bulbs there are tazetta, poeticus and jonquil narcissi, hyacinths and lilies. It is not difficult, when thinking of shrubs, to remember viburnums, daphnes, osmanthus and wintersweet. Dianthus, sweet peas, stocks and nicotianas merely start a long list of perennials and annuals. However, a scent is a scent, whatever kind of plant produces it, and the impact a scent has on us has much to do with how the plant originating it is positioned in the garden. Before going into that, though, let us look at what is by far the largest group of scented plants: the roses.

THE ROLE OF ROSES

Modern rose colours, especially vermilion and the strong yellows, were made possible only by the introduction of *Rosa foetida* and *R. f. bicolor*, a species (once known as *R. lutea*) and form of species in which the genes for such colours were uniquely present. Old roses had a limited palette that consisted mainly of tints and shades from crimson round to violet, and pink tones predominated, along with white. What the old roses had in

Two old-fashioned roses that have benefited from the repeat-flowering tendency of the China Rose. *R. chinensis* 'Mutabilis' has single flowers that open coppery yellow from copper-red buds and then turn pink before deepening to near-crimson. 'Perle d'Or' is similar to 'Cecile Brunner', and has exquisite, small, sweetly fragrant, 'buttonhole' blooms of soft apricot, fading to cream

abundance was scent – several distinct kinds – and interesting, greatly varied flower shapes.

The advent of the bright colours was 'A Good Thing'. However, *Rosa foetida* has, as its name suggests, a slightly unpleasant smell, although many of us cannot detect it, finding it merely scentless. Unfortunately, colours were not the only things it transmitted genetically, and as its descend-

The English Roses are the most significant breakthrough in rose breeding. . . and are set to create a complete revision of how we make up our mixed borders

ants proliferated, so did the numbers of lovely looking, but scentless roses. Many of the old rose scents were almost entirely suppressed, leaving only the 'tea' fragrance, a legacy of the nineteenth century, when it arose from crossing Bourbon roses with 'Hume's Blush China' and 'Parks' Yellow Tea-Scented China'.

Also suppressed were the old-rose flower shapes and their structures as shrubs. The bedding rose reared up like Genghis Khan out of the East and took over, high of bud, pointed of bloom, on an irrelevant bush that had to be cut down every year to act the more efficiently as a bearer of flowers.

Such roses give enormous pleasure all over the temperate world. Gardeners, for whom the slightest hint of miffery or susceptibility to ailments in any other kind of plant is enough to rule it right out, take endless pains over the highly bred invalids they so assiduously cosset. Such roses are thought of simply as roses and are deeply loved, but the wind of change is at hand.

People increasingly want plants that *grow* and do not rise to 90cm (3ft) each year only to have to be cropped back to stumps each winter. They have realised, too, that the proliferation of new rose varieties that takes place each year can be plotted on preference curves whose only coordinates are colour choices. With each year that passes the curves become closer and closer together so that now there is little room for manoeuvre; there is not much more that can be done with colour in roses. That is why the market in rose names has taken off. If your rose is only marginally different, call it after

a TV star and ring up the big bucks.

The reaction to this has been a strong resurgence of interest in the old-fashioned roses and a new desire to grow roses that *grow*. Old-fashioned roses are proper shrubs, complete with scent, but many of them flower only once a year. Modern shrub roses may lack scent but they are shrubs too and play their part in the garden as shrubs, not as amorphous bushes that stick out like sore thumbs. Climbers and ramblers are increasingly popular, as gardeners come to value them for the vertical component they give to the summer garden, at a time when vertical structures – pergolas, porches and walls – are increasingly sought after for their own sakes.

The old-fashioned roses are excellent shrubs for the mixed border, where those that flower only once play as significant a part as any other shrubs, most of which have flowering seasons of less than a month. Their colours go with anything, and crimson gallicas, maturing to parma violet and dove grey in the sun, are happy with a very wide range of companions. Their deep tones are never as lovely as when mingling with the light golden yellow of *Cytisus battandieri*. White and pink Alba roses – 'Mme Legras de St Germain', 'Maiden's Blush', and so on, take very kindly to a carpet of *Lithodora* 'Heavenly Blue', if the soil is lime-free, and are not averse to periwinkle where it is not.

That most deliciously beautiful, early-autumn bulb, *Nerine bowdenii*, planted warmly at the feet of old-fashioned shrub roses, delights in displaying its crystalline-pink flowers against their foliage. Non-repeat flowering is no vice to a gardener who can turn it to his own advantage and let a shrub, once it has flowered, earn its keep in a supporting role. In some ways that is what this book is all about; choosing plants whose presence will be an asset one way or another for far longer than mere flowering takes. In the case of roses, it is probably a matter of personal preference once again; would you rather see Rose 'Piccadilly' flaunting its modern, bicolor blooms non-stop from midsummer to late autumn on a faintly graceless bush, or the Damask rose 'Madame Hardy', shyly covering herself with perfectly cupped, white, exquisitely damask-scented flowers for a month, after which she acts as a graceful backdrop for agapanthus and nerines? Could it be that it is actually better when, 'They are not long, the days of wine and roses'?

English Rose 'The Dark Lady'. The large blooms of this new rose are reminiscent of a tree peony, but have a strong, old-fashioned rose scent

English Rose 'Cottage Rose'. A new rose, and one of the most perpetual-flowering of all. The old-fashioned flowers with a modern colour have a sweet fragrance

English Roses

Recently – starting in the 1960s – a quiet revolution has occurred not very far from Wolverhampton, in the English Black Country. There, a cattle farmer, deeply involved with roses, set out to try the impossible; the marriage between old-fashioned shrub roses and modern forms. His aim was to bring the old-fashioned flower style, the scents, and the shrubby habit of the old roses together with the repeat-flowering and colours of the modern. Relia-bility was to be of the greatest importance, but above all was the aesthetic appeal of the new roses.

David Austin has succeeded beyond his wildest dreams. He no longer farms, but spends his very busy days breeding and assessing his new roses, while he and his son – also David – supervise a mushrooming business, supplying these and other roses to the markets of the world. The English Roses are the most significant breakthrough in rose breeding since the hybrid tea, and are set to create a complete revision of how we make up our mixed borders.

The colours are exquisite, from the rich yellow of 'Graham Thomas', the almost ethereal pink of 'Brother Cadfael', the uniquely perfect shell-blush of 'Heritage', and the white of 'Winchester Cathed-ral' to the apricot-and-yellow of 'Abraham Darby' and the deep crimson of 'Wenlock'. A bouquet of these would waft a succession of distinct perfumes through a large room with never a moment's ennui.

In the garden, these roses are plants of character. They do not take to being bedded out in platoons and battalions, but are best observed as individuals.

Each one, because of its extremely long season, can act as a constant basis for an area of related colour in the mixed border; yellow flowing out from 'Graham Thomas' and 'Jayne Austin', red from the gallica-like crimson of 'William Shakespeare', and pink tones emanating from the clarity of 'Mary Rose'.

Planted like this, or in any way you devise that allows them to be integral elements in your plant-ing, they will take on a rightness that no modern bush rose can. Their perfumes will be an ever-present factor in the impression the garden makes, not only on you, but on everyone who visits it.

Once you have established a high degree of scent among your roses, you can relax, because not every rose then has to have a scent. Still, among modern shrub roses other than the English Roses, there are several that do. 'Cerise Bouquet', for example, has a raspberry fragrance to go with its semi-double flowers. It is once-flowering only, but the pink 'Erfurt', blush-white 'Jacqueline Dupré', and single 'Golden Wings' are among those that are repeat flowering and scented.

CLIMBERS – ROSES AND OTHERS

To return to the positioning of scented plants; it goes almost without saying that you put them where they will be most noticed. *Osmanthus × burkwoodii* or *Viburnum × bodnantense* will be far more effective when planted close by a path or other garden thoroughfare than when tucked away out of nose-reach. Scented jonquils will be wasted if they are in the middle of a drift of narcissi with no scent but which you do not want to trample, and dwarf daphnes are the better appreciated if you do not have to go on hands and knees to them but can sample their perfumes comfortably from a raised bed.

You should differentiate between two classes of perfumed plants; the wafters and the lurkers. Wafters are plants like lilies and roses that drift their scent on the air, sometimes for many yards. Lurkers entrap you by their intriguing looks, drawing you down to them and then belting you with a bolt of scent. *Viola odorata*, *Iris graminea* and *Daphne retusa* are lurkers; dianthus, mignonette and *Daphne bholua* are wafters.

Lurkers should be planted where they may most effectively carry out their life-plan and be brought to the more intimate parts of the garden – seats, urns, raised beds, and by the back door. Wafters will be wasted if you take no notice of the prevailing wind.

It is a shame when scented plants are found at the perimeters of gardens, where their perfumes are blown away in all but the wind from one direction. Someone else gets the benefit, but not their owner. It is much more to the point to concentrate the fragrant plants in the middle of the garden so that you will always be able to find a down-wind spot.

Climbers with scented flowers are not much use, unless they are powerful wafters, if allowed to scramble so far into trees that their nearest flowers are several feet above your head. One of the most pleasant things in a garden is to take a stroll in the soft evening air, while assorted fragrances assail your senses from very close at hand.

Of course, it is not just for scent that we grow climbing plants, but to lend a vertical component to what is essentially a horizontal picture. A wisteria dangling its long, perfumed swags of flowers from a rustic archway is primarily a thing of visual beauty; its scent is secondary. A climbing rose, no matter how deliciously scented, has a part to play in the overall garden picture as well as its role as a bearer of scent.

Climbers help greatly to integrate the house and other features into the garden. Vita Sackville-West's house near Sevenoaks, where she lived before moving to Sissinghurst, is still clad in roses and other climbers in a way that makes it a part of the

garden. As you look from the lowest of the terraces it is as if the garden's gradient suddenly increased and hardly as if there is an abrupt transition from garden to house. In the town garden of André Eve, the famous rose-grower, in Pithiviers, France, there is not a wall to be seen. You emerge from the house into a world of flowers and greenery, where climbers of all sorts, including many climbing and

You emerge from the house into a world of flowers and greenery, where climbers of all sorts, including many climbing and rambling roses, sweep over pergolas and arches and run happily into trees without a care in the world and never allowing a brick to be seen

rambling roses, sweep over pergolas and arches and run happily into trees without a care in the world and never allowing a brick to be seen.

Climbing roses fall broadly into two kinds; older climbers, and the modern ones that are close to hybrid teas and rather short in growth. Some of the 'older' types, like 'Allen Chandler' are hybrid teas, as are 'Climbing Ena Harkness' and 'Climbing Bettina', but we both know what we think of plant categories, don't we? In general, though, climbers have large flowers, either solitary or in small clusters.

They are not very good at sending new growth up from the base and are limited in their height because they have to be pruned annually and those that are repeat-flowering terminate in flower buds and do not go on growing upwards. This applies very much to the modern climbers and renders them less effective, in many ways, than the older ones.

The 'older' climbers are not so old as to be lacking in a wide colour palette or necessarily in scent. 'Dreamgirl', for instance, which dates from 1944, has coral-pink flowers over a long, late season, and has a strong fragrance. It attains a height of 3.3m (10ft). As you might expect, the less remontant 'Crimson Glory' is much taller (half as much again), but it does repeat in short bursts, and its deep crim-

If you can persuade roses to climb trees, you will be able to enjoy far more rose colour than by restricting yourself to growing them in beds and borders. This one was born to blush, not quite unseen, but in a corner of the garden of the Vatican, in Rome

son colour and rich scent are perfect on a pergola.

The most vigorous climbers among this group are the Noisettes, whose flowers are smaller and more in the old style. They are not among the hardiest of roses, but are ideal on warm walls, which they will ascend to heights of 7-8m (22-24ft). The original Noisette, 'Blush Noisette', is not as tall, partly because of its marked repeat-flowering capability, but its semi-double, pink flowers are profusely borne and have the scent of clove pinks. These are genuinely old roses. 'Blush Noisette' was raised by Philippe Noisette, nurseryman, of Charleston, South Carolina, sometime before 1817.

Climbing species are often extremely vigorous and only for large gardens. *Rosa filipes* 'Kiftsgate', for example, grows to over 15m (50ft) high and across in trees – no joke to tidy up after a gale. There is nothing in the whole gardening world, however, to compare with it when in full flower on a summer's day. It is the nearest thing to a floral waterfall that there is.

We are, however, indebted to one climbing species for many of the rambling roses. *Rosa wichuriana* has small, white, scented flowers and vigorous growth. Ramblers in general grow vigorously from the base, cover large areas, and usually flower only once – a good thing, as otherwise they would not make the growth that allows them to scramble so successfully into trees, over walls, and so on.

The colours, with the exceptions of a few, such as 'Alexander Girault', are not strong, but again this makes them ideal for informal scrambling. It does not matter much, either, if some have little scent (although many are beautifully fragrant), as the flowers will, for the most part, be out of range, even when in wafting mode, and would, in any case, be masked by perfumes from roses nearer at hand. They are, without doubt, excellent for making trees become bedecked with roses when otherwise they would just be green.

Clematis – the large-flowered ones – are all too seldom used in this manner, and yet it is the perfect way to grow them. If you have difficulty remembering which should be pruned to within 30cm (1ft) of the ground in early spring and which should merely have their old flower stems removed, you can relax, as it does not matter with clematis that

Clematis seem to be in keeping wherever they are grown, whether climbing freely in a tree or scrambling with carefully controlled rapture over the porch of a cottage

grow into trees. Clematis naturally make flowers at the ends of the growths, where they come into the light, so that the trees look as though there is an outer shell of clematis blooms. The reason for the pruning regimes is to avoid having great lengths of bare stems and to induce flowering much lower down. In trees that becomes unnecessary and you can let nature take its course.

It is best to use deciduous trees, and you should time things so that the flowering of the tree and that of the clematis do not coincide. Beyond that, though, the choice of combinations is, if not infinite, extremely large. It would be tedious to try to give examples, as it is so seldom that a clematis is anything but perfectly appropriate in a tree, but it is not wise to use trees that are too small or too young;

nor do weeping trees look right with clematis dripping from their branches.

Plant your clematis by making a large hole whose nearest edge to the tree is a foot away from it, and put it in on a slant, training it along a cane sloping into the lower branches. Fill the hole with the richest compost you can lay hands on, water copiously, repeating it in dry spells for at least the first three years, and you will have as beautiful a vertical feature as you could wish for – striking, dramatic, and curiously exotic.

Wisterias, so often seen straggling all over a wall in the manner of the Medusa's locks, are superb in trees. The sheer sumptuousness of their great tassels, hanging luxuriantly from and among the branches well over your head, makes for one of the most spectacular sights in gardening. You should employ one with shorter racemes, not the massive *Wisteria* 'Macrobotrys', whose talents are better deployed lower down, as it will look more natural and naturalness is the keynote when climbers run up into trees. Yes, there is not much natural about the larger clematis blooms, but they look right, just the same.

Wisteria floribunda 'Macrobotrys' on a pergola

Perhaps is is because, although we know they are the product of intensive breeding, they look, for the most part, like flowers that nature would have allowed to evolve if she had been given the chance. Clematis seem to be in keeping wherever they are grown, whether climbing freely in a tree or scrambling with carefully controlled rapture over the porch of a cottage.

Nevertheless, they are at their absolute best when growing in company. Clematis never have as much impact as when their flowers seem to erupt from the branches and foliage of other plants without seeming to have any support of their own. This is part of their charm when in trees, but it also helps to explain why they are so spectacular when growing on a wall with a large-leaved ivy. *Hedera colchica* 'Paddy's Pride' – also known as 'Sulphur Heart' because of the central splash of greenish-yellow on the large leaf – and the deep blue-purple of *Clematis* 'The President', complete with its silver reverse, make an unforgettable combination on a wall in late summer.

Clematis and rambling or climbing roses go together because of contrast and tonal order. The small-flowered, summer flowering species clematis are plants for covering unsightly buildings or tumbling down banks; their flowers are of the wrong size and shape and their colours too light for associating with roses, and their extremely vigorous, tangled growth can be a positive danger to arches and pergolas. The large-flowered clematis, however, are perfect for the job, their generally flat, simple flowers the ideal foils for the pointed or cupped roses. Use colours in the blue and purple range, leaving out pink, and the clematis and roses will enhance each others' charms and, furthermore, lend the fascination of texture to the scene.

Texture comes into its own in the vertical component of gardening. Much of what we should be trying to do with trees is a matter of texture, and where plants are climbing upwards, the play of light on them is different from when they are on the flat. The shadows thrown by a rambling rose on itself are of a different nature from those of an ivy or a clematis, and the shapes of flowers and leaves create textures as distinct from one another as are the silk-clad walls in a Duke's mansion and Chinese-restaurant flock.

Much nonsense is talked about texture, usually as a result of trends in art resulting from there being

'Huldine', a clematis whose pearly-white flowers have mauve reverses, tones in well with the orange-pink of a climbing rose, and hitches a lift from it as they scramble upwards together

too many people engaged in it who cannot do it. This disease, which has resulted in 'poetry' that is mere broken-up prose, plays with no plots and music with no notes, has sanctified texture among those who cannot paint. For this reason, there is not much about it in this book. Gardeners who slide down the slippery chute at whose bottom are obsessions with green flowers, the exclusivity of foliage, and academically exact collections of sempervivums, tend also to talk avidly about texture. The truth is that if you see to everything else, texture will look after itself, but when it comes to gardening on walls, pergolas and so on, it is well worth giving it a bit more thought. Don't get trendy about it, though.

For so many gardeners, climbers mean clematis, roses, ivy and wisteria. It is highly understandable; what more could you ask for than such marvellous genera? There are more shots in the climber locker, however, some of which are plants whose presences can be very telling indeed.

For the foliage fans – and others – *Actinidia kolomikta* is a 'must'. When the plant is mature and clothing a wall, its tricolor variegation has a more spectacular effect than most climbers that flower well. The terminal half of each leaf is creamy white with a bright pink flush, and a well grown plant of this twining climber can outdo everything near it on a summer's day.

Then there is *Parthenocissus quinquefolia*, the true Virginia creeper – the one with five-lobed leaves. There is nothing in gardening more remarkable than a large wall bearing an established drapery of its brilliant orange and scarlet in autumn. When the lowering sun of late afternoon plays on it the dazzle is another of those with a hypnotic, but strangely calming effect.

But it is always to scented climbers that we finally turn, as there are few experiences that, for sheer charm, can compete with archways, gateways, alleys and walks where perfume drifts about your head. As you leave the small, intimate Botanic Garden at Pisa, just a short walk from the famous leaning tower, you pass through a door in the high wall and the billowing cloud of jasmine that almost envelops it. It is one of the sweetest farewells in the world, and fitting for one of Europe's most secret, yet most welcoming gardens.

If your wall is a warm one and your climate benevolent, try *Mandevilla suaveolens*, known as the Chilean jasmine, but not a jasmine at all. The scent carried by its white flowers, fully 5cm (2in) across the mouth, is feminine, delicate, subtle and sophisticated. It is easily grown from seed and you can grow it in your conservatory, too.

If the combination of ideas – scent and climbers – sets you off on romantic thoughts of honeysuckle, for heaven's sake do not plant it in company. It is as

Honeysuckle is as rampant a strangler as ever terrorised Boston and should be institutionalised by sentence to solitary confinement

rampant a strangler as ever terrorised Boston and should be institutionalised by sentence to solitary confinement. The local pub near which I once lived had it absolutely right; a muscular honeysuckle twined its woodbine coils over and round an old well-head in the centre of the cobbled courtyard. The power of its perfume was enough triumphantly to overcome the odours of spilled beer and tobacco smoke, and the strength of its grip was known on occasion to detain the odd roué fool enough to try to leave without paying his round.

CHAPTER 7

———◦⌁———

GARDEN FEATURES, ROCKS AND WATER

———◦⌁———

It is not only fine feathers that make fine birds.

AESOP

An artificial pond with a natural appearance that is beautifully contrived. Among the plants are irises, lysichitums and *Alchemilla mollis*, with *Euphorbia griffithii* 'Fireglow' in the middle ground

'Creative gardening' is a battered phrase that has come to mean whatever any given Tweedledum wants it to mean, from pretentious attempts to upgrade simple flower gardening to genuine and valuable revisions of the art of putting plants together. If gardening is to be truly creative – that is to say, if it is to be a satisfying and fulfilling means of self-expression – it must have much to do with balance.

There is a balance between flowers and foliage, another between evergreen and deciduous foliage; and the deployment of light and dark colours needs to be a balanced one. Contrast involves balance, and so does comparison. The harmony found in a well-ordered garden is based on the absence of imbalance.

There is a balance between the plantsman side of the gardener and his designer self. But is there, in the broader world, a balance between the ways in which we are encouraged to use plants and the hard sell of hard landscape? Garden features represent good profits, while plants can die on you, and even the tax people generally allow that 10 per cent of them will not survive to the point of sale. Do you have steps, a 'patio', tubs and urns, dividing walls made of stone trellis, a 'fish pond' (or worse, a 'fish pond and rockery'), a watercourse, paving and raised beds because you really want them, or because somebody has persuaded you that you ought to have them?

Fashions always give rise to backlash when their courses are run. Just as the popularity of hostas is likely to decline dramatically, simply because there are too many similar, unattractively named cultivars on the market, so the over-production of garden features may well lead to their being shunned in the future.

This would be a shame, as so many of them can markedly increase the impact of the plants associated with them. It is all a matter of balance and appropriateness. My wife joyfully regales friends with the anomalies she saw recently in a garden as she was driving by. On a sloping but naturally featureless expanse, a bridge bridged nothing. A pergola stood, forlorn as a long-abandoned temple, not far from a windmill that was laughably out of scale. Walls sprouted from the turf and did nothing but exist. What made it all so sad was that there were no shrubs, trees, or any other plants at all.

It is an extreme example, but salutory. It is all very well to try to emulate Dali or de Chirico in the studio, but it does not work in the garden. Neither does the opposite extreme, in which there are no artefactual features at all. There should be a balance between the garden features and the plants, and it is best achieved when the features emphasise the messages of the plants.

Garden features are statements of the essentially artificial environment; a garden is by definition divorced from the natural. Their function in relation to the plants is to hold them up for inspection, to display the virtues of some of them more fully than is possible otherwise, and sometimes, as in rock and water gardens, to call attention strongly to the environments from which the plants originally came.

If you are looking to create a balanced and unobtrusively 'right' setting for your plants, the setting should be made to suit them, rather than vice versa

If this is attempted but done unsympathetically, the plants may be held up, not to praise, but to ridicule. There is not that great a danger, though, as long as features occur where they might reasonably be expected. A bridge should provide a crossing for a stream or canal, but should also seem to be necessary; it looks silly when a child's step could span it with ease. A wall should at least appear to have a purpose, such as dividing a sitting-out area from the rest of the garden. Steps should occur on what is demonstrably a main thoroughfare, even if it is only made obvious by the contours of the lawn.

Features that are appropriate structurally and functionally are capable of supporting plants that might otherwise be difficult or even impossible. At Bodnant, in North Wales, tender, evergreen magnolias are trained on the balustrades of steps and terraces and live far longer than they would be expected to fully in the open. In a large garden near London that I visited recently, a tall yew hedge was host to fuchsias, *Eccremocarpus scaber* (a Chilean climber with small, orange flowers), *Jasminum polyanthum*, and tropaeolums. The head gardener said that all of them overwintered successfully, year after year. It was interesting, by the way, that pruning the hedge caused little damage to the climbers.

Features that are appropriately placed can support plants that would otherwise not fit in aesthetically. This is precisely because they are artificial. If you love yuccas and cannot find a spot where their extreme spikiness would fit in, give them sentinel duty by an arched gateway or let them occupy an angle between walls. Tall hedges enclosing a small, south-facing enclave will allow you to change the ambience entirely with, say, a cool, informal, leafy, 'English' garden giving way to a hot bright Mediterranean scene where raked gravel, sword-shaped leaves and brilliant colours take over. The hedges, on the other hand, must not be ranged self-consciously like a vegetable squash court, but should relate to the house in a way that makes them entirely to be expected.

Mind you, you should have in your garden precisely what you want in it, including gnomes and antique staddle-stones dating back to 1986 if that is your fancy. But if you are looking to create a balanced and unobtrusively 'right' setting for your plants, the setting should be made to suit them, rather than vice versa.

Of course, you can do little about the house and the general shape of the garden, apart from not having chosen it in the first place. The contours, too,

The small garden cannot take more than one or two strongly delineated features. Any more will create a fiddly fussiness that will destroy all that you have achieved with the plants

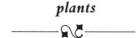

can only be altered in minor ways. What you most definitely can do, though, is to ensure that there is a balance between the needs of the plants, the requirements of family life, and your desire to see certain kinds of features for their own sakes.

POOLS AND ROCKS

You are better off without some garden features than trying to fit them in where there is not enough room and ending up with smaller editions than are convincing. The small garden cannot take more

The charm of a waterside planting is greatly enhanced by the reflections of the plants in the water. Reflections cannot, however, be seen in murky water, which is inevitable if your pond is too small or too shallow. Here Beth Chatto's delightful planting can be enjoyed to the full

than one or two strongly delineated features. Any more will create a fiddly fussiness that will destroy all that you have achieved with the plants. If you cannot make a proper rock garden, for example, incorporate a small, rocky, scree area into your border – as if there were rocks there in the beginning and you had to make the border round them – and you will be able to grow your favourite alpines without having to have an irrelevant excrescence on the place.

Similarly, forget about a pond unless you have room to make one of good size. A small one will clog up with algae and rapidly become anoxic in hot weather. Those fish that do not suffocate will probably die of boredom, and your one water-lily will try to climb out. When the liner finally gives in, you will be only too glad of the excuse to get rid of the whole thing.

The story is told of the nouveau-riche woman who had recently ordered a lake dug in her large garden. Engaging the local lady of the manor in conversation at the fête she asked, 'Do you have swans on your lake too?' To which the swift reply came, 'Only on the smaller one'. It is very difficult to make a stretch of water in the garden large enough to appear natural or even other than just silly.

Perhaps the best way is to incorporate it in or

associate it with a rock garden, but not, please, in the rockery-with-fishpond manner, in which the rockery is so obviously the mound made when the

The placid grace of water-lilies is quite ruined when a couple of inches of bright blue liner show all too clearly that they are growing in a man-made hole in the ground

pond was excavated. Those blue things made of rigid plastic are not terribly convincing, either.

A rock garden should look as if an outcrop of natural rock happened to be a feature of the plot of ground that eventually came to have your house built on it. It should be made of a decent sort of rock, not that awful, shiny, amorphous white gypsum that is sometimes sold as 'rockery stone'. If you go to the hills for a day and study them, you will see that rock outcrops are made up of strata, fissured vertically, and that is how you lay your rocks, not like sultanas on a bun.

The strata rarely lie flat, but usually emerge from the ground at something of an angle. To emulate such naturalness is not difficult; it is largely a matter of butting up the rocks in any one stratum one to another and filling the joints with well-rammed soil, preferably adding a crevice-loving saxifrage, lewisia or campanula as you go. You do not need to make a mound, as you will have incorporated so much organic matter, coarse sand and fine gravel into the soil that it will have the consistency of a slightly moist Christmas-cake mix with extra sugar crystals and will, once the rocks are set, occupy three times its previous volume. The rocks will be set back into the raised soil so that rain runs into the rock garden and not off it, and each rock will have soil rammed so firmly round it that you can stand on it without its rocking. You will end up with a structure that alpines will recognise as a home-from-home, some in crevices, others in pockets, and still others tumbling happily over the rock surfaces.

The impact on the garden and on you will be that of the combination of the rock garden itself and the plants that live in it. It will be an integral part of the garden, not a warty growth on it, and the plants

will appear to have every reason to be there. In short, there will be balance.

An associated pond can be perfectly convincing as long as it looks as though it has been there in terms of geological time as well. The placid grace of water-lilies is quite ruined when a couple of inches of bright blue liner show all too clearly that they are growing in a man-made hole in the ground. Somehow, too, the most artfully constructed 'alpine' pool loses credibility when furnished with a fountain – or worse, one of those endlessly regurgitating, pop-eyed fishes.

PATHS

Paths are the weakness of many gardens. Nature abhors a straight line, but, knowing this, most gardeners fall into the trap of making curves for the sake of not having straight lines. A path that describes a curved course without any apparent reason for it suggests that sobriety is not a priority with those using it. Garden paths should lead unfussily and directly to whatever it is they are aimed at. The secret is that there should, in fact, be goals and not just places where the paths stop.

If a path leads from the back door to the compost heaps, the last thing you will want to do in winter will be to have to steer along an intricately curved

Simple, unfussy paths at Wisley. The magnolia is *M. stellata* 'King Rosea'

path while carrying a load of compostable kitchen waste with the wet branches slapping you in the face as you go. It is much better if your path makes no attempt to wiggle about among the trees and shrubs but goes boldly to one side of them and in a purposeful, graceful curve. By being visible throughout its length, its curve ameliorates the linearity of the garden; if hidden it can corkscrew all it likes and the garden will still look oblong. You would, similarly, become rapidly fed up if your route to the vegetable garden was a thing of dainty curves when all you wanted to do was to get the barrow down there and lift a week's supply of potatoes.

Paths are often impossibly impractical in terms of the materials from which they are made. All sorts of twee 'pavers' (a word nearly as yucky as 'patio' and surpassed only by those ads that plead with

In a situation like this, there could be no alternative to paving. If you want to pave your paths, try for the artistry with which this work was carried out in the garden designed by Gertrude Jekyll and Edward Lutyens at Hestercombe, Somerset, England

Purposefully curved paths

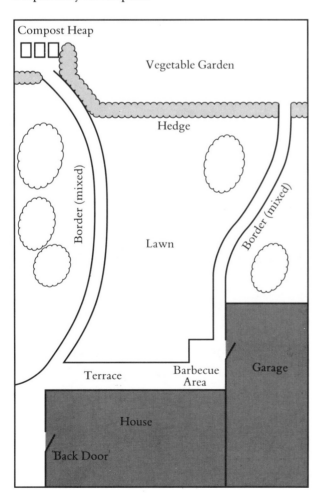

gardeners to wear 'body warmers') are put forward as *le dernier cri* for making paths. We are, for goodness's sake; asked in the same breath to make our paths wondrously curved and also from ornamental bricks!

Paving stones, unless they have very rough surfaces, acquire during the winter a lethal skim of algae, capable of sending a wellington boot flying at little short of Mach 1. You won't have much impact from your rare, near-black hellebores when two hundred pounds of gardener has to spend the flowering season in traction after crushing the things to sappy fibre. Neither will your patience be rewarded when, after waiting for the year when your Mollis azaleas bloom for the first time, the same mass-times-velocity is released violently at them by the protruding lip of a highly expensive Hamburg brick.

The most natural, unobtrusive, easily managed paths are made from what is called 'binding gravel'. It is the gravel that is quarried by sand and gravel merchants, yellow ochre in colour, and you order it simply as 'path gravel'. It should not be washed or

'half-inch down', or anything clean like that, but should have substantial proportions of sand and clay mixed with it.

You loosen the soil where the path is to be, using a fork, and then lay the gravel neatly on top, about 6cm (2½in) deep and rake it level. Then you roll it with a garden roller and leave it to settle for a day or so. It will mature to a light umber and will stand up to endless wear and tear. It is non-slip and non-trip and the plants look marvellous near it, as it is just

Gardens are not natural places, but we can make them as nearly so as possible, otherwise we risk spoiling all the effort we have put into creating gently harmonious groupings of plants

the sort of surface that often occurs in nature. When you think it has become too dirty or worn, tease it loose with a fork, lay 4cm (1½in or so) of gravel on top, roll again, and off you go for another five years.

Among plants, paths absolutely must be natural. Paths between the larger flower beds and borders and those sorts of paths that link features such as lawns or lead from lawns into trees, and especially

A white wisteria, flowering abundantly and growing neatly as a result of having been pruned carefully, thoroughly and at the right time.

paths through trees and among shrubs, should be no more than 'trods' – a word from the north of England denoting the paths made by sheep. They need, however, to be comfortable, dry and safe, and I have found nothing to come anywhere near, let alone surpass, coarsely ground forest bark.

For two years now, the path to my study, which is across an uneven, grassy area from the house, has been a simple trod, surfaced with bark. It passes by rhododendrons, hollies and escallonias and between flag irises and croscosmias. It gets a bit narrow from time to time, as there is insufficient traffic to keep the grass at bay from the sides for very long, but it is only a matter of half an hour's work with the strimmer every few months to keep it in check. It has seen cups of tea, glasses of wine and beer and endless personally precious manuscripts carried along it daily in all weathers, and all kinds of foot-gear from wellies to slippers. It is safe in wet weather and one is footsure in the dark.

These two materials – binding gravel and bark – are as complementary to the plants as you can get. Gardens are parts of our homes and are places where we have to go about our activities, making tracks as we go. They are not natural places, but we can make them as nearly so as possible, otherwise we risk spoiling all the effort we have put into creating gently harmonious groupings of plants by giving them garish or, worse, trendy artefacts among which to languish.

BUILDINGS AND SUNDRY SCAFFOLDS

There are many different ways of growing plants on house walls. First of all, though, you will need to decide whether you want the bother. Plants make decorating very difficult if you have a stucco or pebble-dash finish to the walls, and it is not everyone who can put up with the spiders and other creepies that use climbing plants as ladders to get into warm bedrooms.

The effect of a single clematis, pointlessly wandering up one of those ready-made trellises that occupy relatively small sections of walls, will be the reverse of impressive. So will an improperly pruned, whippy wisteria, seldom flowering but making masses of droopy, unfettered leaf round the guttering as if some Caligula had garlanded it as consul. Plants on walls require more discipline and care than those almost anywhere else.

There is no alternative to providing proper anchorage, and you must be prepared for the plants to grow right to the top of a two-storey house. A narrow strip of trellising – say 60cm (2ft) wide – will accommodate a large-flowered clematis, the rising stem of a wisteria, *Campsis* × *tagliabuana* 'Madame Galen', and the much shorter *Clematis alpina*. Depending on which large clematis you choose, this should provide flowers from mid-spring to early autumn. The trellis will become invisible behind the stems and foliage of the plants, of which the large-flowered clematis will be the only one to need bringing down for pruning. Just how much of it will depend on what kind it is and which pruning régime it demands.

Wisterias, whether on walls, pergolas, arches, or the superstructures of bridges (where they are ideal), need to be pruned properly. In trees, as we have seen, this does not apply because their natural system of flowering suits that environment. Artificially grown, as it were, they must be induced to flower lower down. The way to do this is to prune during the height of summer, taking all the whippy new growths back to two buds. This will induce

flowering spurs for the following year. You can, if you like, take a second to commit to memory that summer pruning is for flowering; winter pruning is for growth. This applies to fruit trees as much as to ornamentals. If you prune your wisteria only in winter it will become a sadistic tangle of lashes, waiting for the least chance to catch you wickedly across the face as you pass by.

Arches, pergolas, and so on, are structures you put up usually because you fancy them and seldom because they are necessary. They are frankly artificial things, but when erected sensibly they lend charm, shelter, and a considerable degree of intimacy to the garden.

The matter of balance between naturalness – which is what you try to achieve with the plants if you are not gardening formally – and artifice is a tenuous one. If there is a dictum that can be formulated concerning garden structures it must have to do with their raisons d'être. The 'goes-nowhere'

The 'goes-nowhere' pergola is the classic example of sore-thumb artificiality, but a pergola that has some logic to it can soon become a great asset, providing a good, disciplined home for plants. . . and adding another dimension to the garden as a whole

pergola is the classic example of sore-thumb artificiality, but a pergola that has some logic to it can soon become a great asset, providing a good, disciplined home for plants, an excellent means of enjoying them to the full (from the inside as well as out, in a way), and adding another dimension to the garden as a whole. Arches do this too, but 90 per cent of all garden arches are illogical sore thumbs, permissible in a formal parterre or potager, but distinctly odd in the informal garden. Where arches work is where they seem as though they had to be put up in order to carry the plants over the heads of those walking on the path beneath. This works well when a tree by the path has a climbing plant growing through it that is trained out onto the arch. This makes the connection, and you can then grow other plants over it as well, just as you would with an isolated arch.

Controlled profusion – wisteria growing naturally through a laburnum-clad arch, which draws the eye to the seat beyond. A garden feature with a purpose

It would be a mistake, though, to imagine that gardening is ruled by immutable laws. As has been said repeatedly throughout this book, you should feel able to do your own thing in your own garden without fear or favour. There are as many ways and styles of gardening as there are individual gardeners; certain principles obtain and are worth following – other than that the matter of flair comes in. If there is a way that occurs to you of making plants more effective, try it. If you do not like it, you can scrap it again. An example of this is the wigwam method of inducing extra flowering in certain types of roses – ramblers and climbers among them. A wigwam of tall canes is made so that its base is quite wide. The rose stems are then trained in flat spirals round them. The resulting reduction in the flow of sap induces flowering all along the stems and not just at their tops. The same idea is used at the Roseraie de l'Hay in Paris, France, where roses are trained along swagged ropes. The wigwam method is used at the College of Horticulture and Agriculture in Dorset, England, where the wigwams are at regular intervals in what otherwise is quite an informal border. It is a show-stopping spectacle that may well be unorthodox, but is nevertheless highly effective.

LAWNS, CONTOURS AND OUTLINES

If you have a lawn, and most people have, it is arguably the most important element in the whole garden when it comes to the impact that the plants will have. You can follow the principles of related planting, choosing plants with character, observing tonal order and everything else, but if your lawn is poorly done you might as well not have bothered.

Because the lawn is green it is a reservoir of peace to the eye. Break up the greenness with patches of wear, disturb the eye with uneven bumpiness and tattily neglected grass, offend with frayed edges, and the effect is ruined. The great paradox is that lawns are highly artificial but play to perfection a natural part. Only the smooth, frequently mown sward, neatly edged and kept from wearing out, can act as a foil and companion for artfully arranged plants. Perhaps the reason is that, no matter how we try, a garden is essentially artificial and we need the lawn as a bridge between the severe structures of house, fences, hedges, walls and paths – and the freer ambience of the plants. Visit a garden with no lawn and you may sense an uneasiness between house and garden; go to another where there is one, even if quite small in relation to the amount of garden, and the house and garden seem more at ease with one another.

The same effect can be gained by using stretches

of gravel – a lawn is not *de rigueur* – but the therapeutic greenness will be absent. You may feel that a yearly application of pre-emergent weedkiller is infinitely preferable to the tyranny of the lawn mower, and who is to deny it, but all those millions cannot be wrong; most of us like our lawns.

The edge of the lawn is the interface between it and the areas where plants are growing. You may think that is a jargonistic way of saying, 'lawns have edges', but there is more to it than that. The interface is one of the most important features in the garden. It outlines the shape of the lawn and determines the shapes of the beds. It is the means whereby the squareness of most gardens is made less demanding on the eye when it describes curves. The curved interface, rather than the garden boundary, becomes, when strongly and unfussily drawn, the dominant surface line.

The shapes thus outlined are intimately part of what gives plants their impact. Other shapes within them – a raised bed within a larger border, for example – do not have the same fundamental

The edge of the lawn. . . becomes, when strongly and unfussily drawn, the dominant surface line. The shapes thus outlined are intimately part of what gives plants their impact

authority. Even a boldly made rock garden, unless it has been made as a lawn feature (an excellent measure, by the way), will be part of the shape drawn by the lawn's edge.

When you realise just what a vital part the edges of the lawn have to play, there can surely be no doubt left as to the necessity of keeping them neatly trimmed. This applies throughout the year – ragged edges will spoil the impact of snowdrops, cyclamen and crocuses just as much as anything else.

The contours of the lawn are usually something about which you can do little without either too much expense or an unwelcome prospect of hard labour. They matter, though. A softly undulating lawn marries better to informal plantings and can be cut away here and there on the downslopes to make sunny rock outcrops or just shallowly sloping, curved beds. Lawn specimens of trees and shrubs

look more natural in undulating lawns, on the same general principle as that followed when making an outcrop rock garden – in other words, the lawn looks as though it was made round the pre-existing tree.

BITS AND PIECES

If the basic structure of the garden is sound, it can absorb the oddments that go with family life without their obtruding. You have probably visited the sort of home where the garden, no matter how tidily kept, is rendered a tip by just a few toys, the odd toddler's tricycle and a ball or two. If you go again, notice how little there is to draw your eye away from them. The garden is probably flat, meagrely planted, and with a lawn whose design turns its back on itself.

Now think of the gardens you have been to where the families are busy and cheerful but the gardens always look serene despite the presence of strewn teddies and the sorts of plastic gewgaws that glare shinily in the sun. What is the difference? It is that you keep wanting to look away towards the colours and shapes of the plants. The garden is so made that the family will grow up in it much as it is now, except that the plants will too. In the first sort of garden there is a temporary atmosphere, as if the tents are about to be struck as the tribe moves on to another oasis. In the second there is a feeling of roots, an imperturbable sense of home and belonging; peace and tranquillity, dollies and roller skates notwithstanding.

It follows that, given firmness of structure and the intriguing durability that harmony brings, you can afford to indulge in raised beds, tubs, urns, steps, bowers, fountains and, within limits, whatever else you desire. In a garden with little real plant interest, such things intrude. They break up what must be kept utterly simple if it is to work at all, whereas the other type of garden can take interruption without the occurrence of distraction.

To populate your garden with plants whose presence is well and truly felt – in many cases all year round – and to integrate them into a sympathetic setting, is to create something more than just a good garden. It is to extend to the outdoor environment the peace and security of home, than which there is nothing in life more valuable.

A NOTE ON CULTIVATION

It is not of the slightest significance how many basic principles of planting we have learned to follow, how subtly artistic with colour we may have become, or how many books we have read (or written); it will all go for nothing if we do not practise good cultivation.

Poor cultivation makes nonsense of plant descriptions. It is no good blaming the nurseryman if the plants do not come up to expectation, and pointless to argue with gardening writers that their descriptions bear no relation to reality, if your standards of cultivation make it impossible for the wish and the reality to coincide.

A badly grown plant will have no impact. Bad cultivation prevents the proper production of pigment, colour values fall off and sometimes change radically. Badly nourished foliage cannot impress with its boldness or delicate laciness, and trees that should be noble barely make it to ranks of the bourgeois. Flowering may be dangerously profuse, but it is likely to be the reaction of a plant facing imminent death; enjoy the moment, it is unlikely to recur. Seeds will be set sparsely if at all, internodal growth will be too short for cuttings to be taken, and you will lose your plants while being unable to propagate them.

Good cultivation produces lusty plants, enthusiastic in their displays of leaf, flower and form, and capable of shrugging off attacks of disease. Colour saturation is good, the hues and tones as they should be, seed is set prolifically and germinates readily, while cuttings root with avidity.

Good cultivation is that which promotes health and vigour in plants. The two most essential elements of it are food and a sense of the space needed by the plants. Starvation, which occurs in more gardens than you might care to know about, and overcrowding kill more plants than do the pests

and diseases that would otherwise be resisted.

'Food' implies other things than mere nutrition. Lack of oxygen destroys a plant's ability to feed itself, and so does lack of water. Paradoxically, an excess of water excludes oxygen from the soil. Good drainage is utterly vital; without it, forget it.

The texture of the soil can itself inhibit drainage and the uptake of water and nutrients. It can also lead to the rapid onset of drought conditions and to the rupture of roots when clay soils crack in the dry. The liberal addition of well-rotted organic matter is the surest way to improve any soil. It greatly alleviates the effects of drought and soil movement and makes a congenial home for the teeming soil fauna which are so vital for the well-being of anything growing in it.

It also provides most of the food that plants need, apart from that made by the action of light on the leaves, but even then the green pigment that does the job relies on the soil for atoms vital to its molecule. Generous applications of organic matter make for richly green leaves, intensely coloured flowers, and for the defeat of fungi and insect predators.

Town dwellers often complain that they cannot obtain organic matter. Of course they can. The riding schools are often desperate to get rid of the piles of manure that grow faster than you would credit, and park keepers will, if approached nicely, often part with autumn leaves, which you can take away in bags for rotting down. If all else fails, buy a dozen or so bales of straw and pile them up to rot down. If you can manage a little success from each source, throw them all together and let them turn gradually to an amorphous, black, gorgeous and thoroughly satisfying compost.

A good mulch of compost, bark, or any other suitable organic material, applied every spring or

autumn, whenever you have the materials and time, will work wonders in keeping the soil from drying, as well as providing food for the plants and work for the worms. A little bone-meal spread at the same time will do no harm, but that should be all that is necessary if the general organic element is as copious as possible.

Hygiene is a matter of tidiness. Bits of wood left around attract pests and fungi, especially the dread honey fungus. You are likely to have some honey fungus in your garden anyway (it is everywhere), but there is no sense in inviting it to become actively predatory. Pruning should remove all dead, dying and diseased wood as a matter of routine, and it should be burned, not put on the compost heap or left in a pile in a corner.

The good cultivator will have an eye to the deterioration of a previously good situation. This sort of thing occurs, for example, when routine garden operations or the family's foot-traffic cause compaction of the soil. Aeration of the lawn helps, but if there is a definite track, put large, flat stones (crazy paving – not 'pavers'), stepping-stone fashion, about 2.5cm (1in) below grass-level and mow right over their edges. In the border, notice where you most usually stand or stoop to weed and tend the plants, and put down stepping stones at those places. They will distribute the pressure created by your weight so that at any given point on the soil it is a fraction of what it would be if your entire weight were felt there.

When pests and diseases do strike, your vigilance should ensure that the attack has minimal effect. This is not the place for a catalogue of remedies; it is rather in the spirit of the book to suggest to you that your love for and consequent involvement with the plants you have chosen and placed so carefully will keep you constantly alert to anything that might harm them. The health of your plants will be ensured to a considerable extent by the presence within you of the soul of a plantsman and the ambition of a designer.

GAZETTEER OF PLANTS

The lists that follow are not meant to be even remotely comprehensive. Neither do they give all the information necessary to grow the plants. They are designed merely to whet your appetite and to give you an idea of which are some of the best and most effective plants among those generally available to gardeners.

They are also all plants of which I have first-hand experience, and this seemed to be as good a criterion as any other for determining how long the lists should be. Perhaps it has made them too short, but I have left out other plants that, although worth growing, are not the first ones you think of in the same breath as 'impact'.

You may find it a little odd that *Musa basjoo* – a banana from Japan – is included. Perhaps it is, but it is easily grown from seed, stands up to winters outside in mild areas if its leaves are tied up so that they do not thrash about in the wind, and is, if grown in a tub that is put outside in the summer, quite the most atmospheric plant of all. You may also think it rather commonplace to include a foxglove. Maybe so, but the flowers of *Digitalis* × *mertonensis* (which is a seed strain) are of a crushed strawberry tint that, as far as I know, is possessed by no other flower.

Choice has, though, been difficult. Large genera have been dealt with in different ways. For example, the whole gamut of *Camellia* has been covered with two entries, *Rhododendron* gets a piece to itself, and *Clematis* is similarly singled out. Where just about all the named forms – as in *Delphinium* – are equally good and choice depends on which colours you like, the entry is a blanket one. Where there are just one or two that are really outstanding, they are the only ones named.

A few bulbs are listed with perennials. In the main, however, they have been omitted from the lists, as to choose just a few daffodils, for example, would be invidious and would tend to be restricting. There are few bad daffodils, crocuses and tulips, so your choice is far wider than any list I might make.

Consistent with my insistence throughout the book on the value of research, I hope that the lists will lead you to seek further information from among the works cited in the bibliography, and that they will enrich your gardening as much as they have mine.

A NOTE ON PLANT NAMES

Until the eighteenth century plants were described, rather than named. Such orotund designations as *Tulipa globosa serotina aureo colore punctata* and *Hyacinthus stellatus Aquitanicus coeruleo flore* were the norm, and life must have been increasingly complicated for botanists, herbalists and gardeners.

Carl von Linné (1707-1778), known as Linnaeus, put a stop to all that by his invention of the binomial system of naming. Instead of being identified by long phrases, plants now had names consisting of two parts, the first of which was the name of the genus to which it belonged, while the second was the epithet that distinguished its species.

Life being what it is, things could not remain that simple for long, and we found ourselves faced with the necessity for further elaboration. Species now are sometimes subdivided into categories called subspecies, forma, or varietas, abbreviated as ssp., f., and var. respectively.

Trinomials are not desirable. Nevertheless in this book I have ignored ssp., f., and var. on two grounds. One is that they are only of real interest to botanists, certain professional horticulturists and highly advanced, usually specialist, amateurs. The

Abutilon × milleri, an exotic shrub for a warm wall

adhered to at every mention of the plant. You will find 'Senkaki' referred to once in a colloquial way, but you will not find dangling, knowing references to specific epithets or vernacular names without first having been alerted to their full status.

I believe that we should use plant names in order to communicate. While it is true that science demands more precision than gardening does, for gardeners it is the God-given beauty of plants that matters, rather than their exact places in man-made taxonomy. We can be glad that this is so, as there are few things more ephemeral than the 'correct' name of a plant.

other is that it is better to leave them out than to get them wrong. As I am just a gardener and not a botanist, I do not normally research into botanical minutiae and thus could not vouch for the accuracy of such terms if I used them. Accordingly, you will find *Berberis thunbergii atropurpurea*, among others, given an apparent trinomial.

I have also used the term 'variety' loosely. In other words, it is used in this book to cover both naturally occurring varieties and cultivars. As the term 'cultivar' is very badly defined anyway, I feel it is better not used until its precise meaning is internationally settled. Furthermore, there is considerable confusion in the literature concerning many plants.

Convention dictates that after the mention of a species, its name should be written as an abbreviation before every subsequent mention of any cultivars. Thus one of the varieties of *Acer palmatum* is written as *A. p.* 'Senkaki'. It can confuse or even destroy the sense of a paragraph in which this is not initially done, but it is, in a gardening book, mere pedantry and an obstacle to free reading when it is

Key
Plant classification   sp = species (singular)   spp = species (plural)   hybs = hybrids   vars = varieties
Tree or shrub   T = tree   Sh = shrub   S-Sh = subshrub   T/Sh = tree or shrub
Flowers   Sp = spring   Sum = summer   Aut = autumn   E.Sp = early spring   L.Sp = late spring   M.Sp = mid spring
Sp-Sum = from spring to summer (ie part of spring and part of summer)   Sp & Sum = most of spring and most of summer   Sp/Sum = spring or summer (some varieties flower in spring, others in summer)
Hardiness   1 = fully hardy   3/4 = hardy except in the coldest districts   1/2 = hardy only in mild areas
Size   D = dwarf   S = small   M = medium   L = large   V = very large
Sun or shade   Sh = shade   P.Sh = partial shade

PERENNIALS	Flower Season	Flower Colour	Scent	Evergreen	Foliage	Coloured Foliage	Fruit/ Seed heads	Sun or Shade	Height and Spread cm (in)	Comments
Acanthus mollis	L.Sum	Pink			•			Sun	120 x 90 (48 x 36)	
Acanthus spinosus	L.Sum	Lilac			•			Sun	120 x 60 (48 x 24)	
Achillea 'Galaxy Hybrids'	Sum	Various			•			Sun	60 x 60 (24 x 24)	
Aconitum 'Sparks Variety'	Sum	Dark Blue						Sun	120 x 50 (48 x 20)	
Aconitum 'Arendsii'	E.Aut	Blue						Sun	120 x 40 (48 x 15)	
Agapanthus 'Headbourne Hybrids'	L.Sum/E.Aut	Blue, White			•		•	Sun	Max 120 x 60 (48 x 24)	
Alchemilla mollis	E.Sum	Yellow-Green			•			Sun	50 x 60 (20 x 24)	
Allium cernuum	Sum	Amethyst					•	Sun	50 x 15 (20 x 5)	Bulb
Allium christophii	Sum	Metallic Amethyst					•	Sun	50 x 50 (20 x 20)	Bulb
Allium giganteum	Sum	Lilac					•	Sun	120 x 30 (48 x 10)	Bulb
Allium 'Purple Sensation'	Sum	Red-Purple					•	Sun	120 x 30 (48 x 10)	Bulb
Alstroemeria 'Ligtu Hybs'	Sum	Varied						Sun	120 x 50 (48 x 20)	
Amaryllis belladonna vars	L.Sum/E.Aut	Pink-Rose	•		•			Sun	60 x 40 (24 x 15)	Bulb not for cold areas
Anchusa 'Loddon Royalist'	E.Sum	Blue						Sun	90 x 60 (36 x 24)	
Anenome x hybrida (syn *A. japonica*)	Aut	Various			•			P. Sh	150 x 60 (60 x 24)	
Aruncus dioicus	Sum	Cream			•			P. Sh	180 x 120 (70 x 48)	
Aster frikartii 'Mönch'	Sum-Aut	Lavender-Blue						Sun	90 x 50 (36 x 20)	
Astilbe x arendsii vars	Sum	Various			•			Sun/P. Sh	60 x 100 (24 x 40)	
Bergenia spp & hybs	Sp	Red, Pink, White		•	••	•		Sun/P. Sh	Max 60 x 60 (24 x 24)	
Brunnera macrophylla vars	Sp	Blue			•	•		P. Sh	50 x 60 (20 x 24)	
Campanula 'Burghaltii'	Sum	Grey-Blue						Sun	50 x 30 (20 x 10)	
Campanula lactiflora	E.Sum/L.Aut	Lilac-Blue						Sun	120 x 50 (48 x 20)	
Campanula persicifolia	Sum	Lilac-Blue						Sun	90 x 30 (36 x 10)	
Canna Hybrids	L.Sum-Aut	Red, Orange, Yellow			••	••		Sun	120 x 60 (48 x 24)	Lift for winter
Chrysanthemum maximum vars	Sum	White						Sun	90 x 50 (36 x 20)	
Chrysanthemum Korean Hybrids	Aut	Various						Sun	60 x 50 (24 x 20)	Hardy
Cimicifuga racemosa	Sum	White			•			Sun	90 x 60 (36 x 24)	
Cimicifuga ramosa 'Atropurpurea'	Aut	White			•	•		Sun	200 x 120 (80 x 48)	
Convallaria majalis 'Fortin's Giant'	L.Sp	White	•		•			P. Sh	50 x 50 (20 x 20)	
Crinum x powellii	Sum	Pink, White	•		•			Sun	120 x 90 (48 x 36)	Bulb
Crocosmia hybs	L.Sum/E.Aut	Various			•			Sun	90 x 25 (36 x 8)	
Delphinium – named hybs	Sum	Various			•			Sun	120 x 90 (48 x 36)	
Dianthus – Garden Pinks	Sum	Various	•	•	•			Sun	Various	
Diascia rigescens	E.-L.Sum	Pink			•			Sun	50 x 50 (20 x 20)	
Diascia 'Ruby Field'	E.Sum/Aut	Pink						Sun	30 x 40 (10 x 15)	
Dicentra formosa	L.Sp-E.Sum	Mauve-Pink			•			P. Sh	50 x 50 (20 x 20)	
Digitalis x mertonensis	Sum	Crushed Strawberry						P. Sh	60 x 30 (24 x 10)	
Echinacea 'Robert Bloom'	Sum	Cerise-Crimson						Sun	100 x 50 (40 x 20)	
Echinops ritro	L.Sum	Blue					•	Sun	120 x 50 (48 x 20)	
Erigeron 'Darkest of All'	Sum	Violet						Sun	60 x 60 (24 x 24)	
Eryngium x oliverianum	Sum	Blue			•	•		Sun	60 x 60 (24 x 24)	
Euphorbia characias	E.Sp	Yellow-Green		•	•		•	P. Sh	120 x 90 (48 x 36)	
Filipendula purpurea 'Alba'	Sum	White	•		•			Sun	120 x 60 (48 x 24)	Waterside
Galtonia candicans	L.Sum	White	•					Sun	120 x 30 (48 x 10)	Bulb
Geranium x magnificum	E.Sum	Violet-Blue			•			Sun	60 x 60 (24 x 24)	
Geranium wallichianum 'Buxton's Blue'	Sum, Aut	Blue			•			Sun	30 x 90 (10 x 36)	
Gunnera manicata	E.Sum	Brown-Green			••			P. Sh	200 x 200 (48 x 48)	Waterside
Helenium 'Butterpat'	E.Aut	Soft Yellow						Sun	120 x 50 (48 x 20)	
Helianthus 'Loddon Gold'	L.Sum	Yellow						Sun	90 x 50 (36 x 20)	
Helleborus orientalis & hybs	Wint-E.Sp	Various			•		•	P. Sh	45 x 60 (17 x 24)	
Hemerocallis hybs	Sum	Various			•			S/P.Sh	90 x 60 (36 x 24)	
Heracleum mantegazzianum	Sum	White			•		•	S/P.Sh	300 x 180 (120 x 70)	
Heuchera 'Palace Purple'	Sum	Copper			•	•		Sun	90 x 150 (36 x 60)	
Hosta spp & vars	Sum, Aut	Lilac, Violet or White			••	••		S/P.Sh	Various	
Iris chrysographes 'Margot Holmes'	E.Sum	Deep Crimson			•			P. Sh	60 x 30 (24 x 10)	
Iris pallida 'Variegata'	E.Sum	Blue			•	•		Sun	90 x 30 (36 x 10)	
Iris pseudacorus 'Variegata'	E.Sum	Yellow			•	•		Sun	100 x 30 (40 x 10)	Moisture
Iris sibirica & vars	E.Sum	Various			•			Sun	90 x 50 (36 x 20)	Moisture
Kniphofia spp & vars	Sum-E.Aut	Various			•			Sun	Max 120 x 60 (48 x 24)	

PERENNIALS	Flower Season	Flower Colour	Scent	Evergreen	Foliage	Coloured Foliage	Fruit/ Seed heads	Sun or Shade	Height and Spread cm (in)	Comments
Ligularia dentata 'Desdemona'	Sum	Orange			•	•		Sun/P.Sh	120 x 60 (48 x 24)	Moisture
Lobelia cardinalis	L.Sum	Red			•			Sun	90 x 30 (36 x 10)	
Lobelia 'Bees Flame'	L.Sum	Red			•	••		Sun	90 x 30 (36 x 10)	Mulch over winter
Lychnis chalcedonica	E.Sum	Vermillion						Sun	90 x 30 (36 x 10)	
Lysichitum americanum	E.Sp	Yellow			••			Sun	120 x 120 (48 x 48)	Waterside
Lysichitum camtschatcense	E.Sp	White			••			Sun	90 x 90 (36 x 36)	Waterside
Malva moschata alba	Sun	White						P. Sh	90 x 60 (36 x 24)	
Meconopsis betonicifolia	E.Sum	Blue or White			•		•	P. Sh	90 x 50 (20)	No lime
Meconopsis grandis	E.Sum	Blue			•		•	P. Sh	90 x 60 (36 x 24)	No lime
Meconopsis x sheldonii	E.Sum	Blue			•		•	P. Sh	120 x 60 (48 x 24)	No lime
Melianthus major	E.Sum	Chocolate	•		••			Sun	120 x 120 (48 x 48)	Tender
Musa basjoo	L.Sum	Brown			••			Sun	180 x 150 (70 x 60)	Mild areas
Nepeta faasenii	All Sum	Lavender			•	•		Sun	50 x 50 (20 x 20)	
Nerine bowdenii	Aut	Pink			•			Sun	50 x 50 (20 x 20)	Bulb, not cold areas
Osteospermum vars	Sum-Aut	Various						Sun	30 x 30 (10 x 10)	Mild areas
Paeonia spp & hybs	L.Sp/E.Sum	Various	•		•	•	•	Sun	Most are 60 x 60 (24 x 24)	
Papaver orientale	E.Sum	Various			•			Sun	Up to 120 x 60 (48 x 24)	
Penstemon 'Garnet'	Sum-Aut	Red			•			Sun	75 x 60 (30 x 24)	
Phlox paniculata vars	L.Sum	Various	•					Sun	120 x 60 (48 x 24)	
Phormium tenax	Sum	Red		•	••		•	Sun	300 x 200	
Phormium tenax 'Purpureum'	Sun	Red		•	••	••	•	Sun	300 x 200 (120 x 80)	
Phormium tenax 'Variegatum'	Sum	Red		•	••	••	•	Sun	300 x 200 (120 x 80)	
Podophyllum hexandrum	Sp	Pink & White			•	•	•	P.Sh	50 x 30 (20 x 10)	Edible fruit
Potentilla 'Gibsons Scarlet'	All Sum	Scarlet			•			Sun	50 x 50 (20 x 20)	
Primula, Candelabra Section	E.Sum	Various			•			Sun/P.Sh	90 x 50 (36 x 20)	Moisture
Primula florindae	Sum	Yellow			•			P.Sh	75 x 50 (30 x 20)	Moisture
Pulmonaria saccharata	Sp	Blue			••	••		P. Sh	30 x 50 (10 x 20)	
Rheum alexandrae	E.Sum	Cream Bracts			••			P. Sh	90 x 60 (36 x 24)	
Rheum palmatum 'Atrosanguineum'	E.Sum	Red			••	••		P. Sh	160 x 160 (64 x 64)	
Rodgersia aesculifolia	Sum	Creamy Pink			••	••		P. Sh	120 x 60 (48 x 24)	
Rodgersia pinnata	Sum	Pink			••	••		P. Sh	90 x 60 (36 x 24)	
Rodgersia podophylla	Sum	White			••	••		P. Sh	90 x 60 (36 x 24)	
Salvia patens 'Cambridge Blue'	Sum-Aut	Cambridge Blue						Sun	50 x 30 (20 x 10)	Mild areas, Mulch
Saxifraga fortunei 'Wadas Variety'	Aut	White			••	••		P. Sh	50 x 30 (20 x10)	
Schizostylis coccinea & vars	E.Aut	Pink-Red						Sun	60 x 30 (24 x 10)	
Sedum spectabile	L.Sum	Mauve-Pink	•		•	•	•	Sun	50 x 50 (20 x 20)	Butterflies
Sedum 'Autumn Joy'	E.Aut	Pink-Red			•	•		Sun	60 x 60 (24 x 24)	No butterflies
Senecio cineraria 'White Diamond'	Insig				••	••		Sun	60 x 60 (24 x 24)	Perennial in mild areas
Smilacina racemosa	Sp	White	••		•			Sh	70 x 50 (28 x 20)	No lime
Solidago 'Goldenmosa'	Sum	Yellow						Sun	90 x 90 (36 x 36)	
x Solidaster 'Lemore'	Sum-Aut	Yellow						Sun	60 x 50 (24 x 20)	
Stachys byzantina 'Silver Carpet'	None	None			••	••		Sun	Ground-Cover	
Symphytum x uplandicum 'Variegatum'	Sp	Lilac-Pink			••	••		Sun	120 x 120 (48 x 48)	Reversion
Thalictrum aquilegiifolium	E.Sum	Lilac			•			Sun	90 x 30 (36 x 10)	
Thalictrum diffusiflorum	Sum	Lilac			••			Sun	90 x 30 (36 x 10)	
Trillium chloropetalum	Sp	Obtain Red Forms	•		••			P. Sh	60 x 30 (24 x 10)	
Trillium grandiflorum	Sp	White			•			P. Sh	40 x 30 (15 x 10)	
Tropaeolum polyphyllum	Sum	Yellow			••	••		Sun	Sprawls	
Veratrum nigrum	Sum	Maroon			••		•	P. Sh	180 x 80 (70 x 30)	
Zantedeschia aethiopica 'Crowborough'	Sum	White			•			P. Sh	120 x 60 (48 x 24)	Waterside

TREES AND SHRUBS

TREES AND SHRUBS	Tree or Shrub	Flowers	Scent	Evergreen or Deciduous	Foliage	Coloured Foliage	Autumn Colour	Shape	Bark (Stems)	Twigs (Branches)	Fruit	Hardiness	Size	Spring	Summer	Autumn	Winter	Comments
Abelia schumannii	Sh	Sum–Aut	•	D	•							1	M		•	•		
Acer capillipes	T			D	•		•		•	•		1	S	•	•	•	•	
Acer griseum	T			D	•		•		••	••		1	S	•	•	•	•	
Acer negundo 'Flamingo'	T/Sh			D	••	•						1	S-M	•	•	•		
Acer palmatum Varieties	T/Sh			D	••	•	••					1	S-M	•	•	•		
Acer palmatum 'Senkaki'	T/Sh			D	••	•	••			••		1	S-M	•	•	•		
Acer palmatum 'Osakazuki'	T/Sh			D	••		•••					1	S-M	•	•	•		
Acer pensylvanicum	T			D	•		••		•			1	M	•	•	•	•	
Amelanchier lamarckii	T/Sh	Sp		D	•	•	•				•	1	M	•		•	•	No lime
Arbutus x andrachnoides	T/Sh	Aut–Wint	•	E	•				••	••		3/4	M	•	•	•	•	
Artemisia 'Powis Castle'	Sh	None		D	••	•						1	S	•	•	•		
Berberis darwinii	Sh	Sp		E	•						•	1	M	•	•	•	•	
Berberis x lologensis	Sh	Sp		E	•						•	1	M	•	•	•	•	
Berberis x ottawensis 'Superba'	Sh	Sp		D	•	•	•	•			•	1	M	•	•	•		
Berberis x stenophylla vars	Sh	Sp		E	•	•		•			•	1	S-M	•	•	•		
Berberis x thunbergii vars	Sh	Sp		D	•	•	•					1	S-M	•	•	•		
Betula albo-sinensis	T			D	•		•		••	•		1	M	•	•	•	•	
Betula ermanii	T			D	•		•		••	•		1	L	•	•	•	•	
Betula utilis jacquemontii	T			D	•		•		••		•	1	M	•	•	•	•	
Callicarpa bodinieri giraldii	Sh	Sp		D	•			•			•	1	S-M	•	•	•	•	
Calluna vulgaris vars	Sh	All year		E	••	•		•				1	S	•	•	•	•	No lime
Camellia japonica vars	Sh	Sp		E	•			•				3/4	M	•	•	•	•	No lime
Camellia x williamsii vars	Sh	Sp		E	•			•				1	M	•	•	•	•	No lime
Ceanothus sp & vars	Sh	Sp Sum		E D	•			•				3/4-1/2	M-L	•	•	•	•	
Ceratostigma plumbaginoides	Sh	L. Sum		1/2E			•	•				1	S	•	•	•		
Choisya ternata	Sh	Sp Aut	•	E	•			•				3/4	S-M	•	•	•	•	
Colletia armata	Sh	L. Sum Aut	•	Leafless				•				1	M	•	•	•	•	
Convolvulus cneorum	Sh	Sp–Aut		E	••	•		•				3/4-1	S	•	•	•	•	
Cordyline australis	T	Sum	•	E	••			•		••		1/2	L	•	•	•	•	Mild areas only
Cornus alba vars	Sh			D	•	•	•			••		1	M	•	•	•	•	
Cornus controversa 'Variegata'	T/Sh	Sp		D	••	•		•		•		1	M	•	•	•		Not on chalk
Cornus florida Group	T/Sh	Sp		D	•		•	•				3/4-1	M	•	•	•		Not on chalk
Cornus kousa chinensis	T	E. Sum		D	•		•	•			••	1	M	•	•	•		
Cotinus coggygria & vars	Sh	Sum		D	•	•	•	•		•	•	1	M	•	•	•		
Cotoneaster (many)	Sh	E. Sum		E D	•		•	•			•••	1	S,M,L	•	•	•	•	

TREES AND SHRUBS

Name	Tree or Shrub	Flowers	Scent	Evergreen or Deciduous	Foliage	Coloured Foliage	Autumn Colour	Shape	Bark (Stems)	Twigs (Branches)	Fruit	Hardiness	Size	Spring	Summer	Autumn	Winter	Comments
Crataegus x lavallei 'Carrierei'	T	Sp-E.Sum		D-½E	•			•			••	1	S	•	•	•	•	Fruit all winter
Crataegus monogyna	T/Sh	Sp-E.Sum	•	D							••	1	S-M	•	•	•	•	
Cytisus battandieri	Sh	Sum	••	D-½E	••	•						1	L	•	•	•		
Daphne (many)	Sh	E.Sp-M.Sum	••	E D	•							3/4-1	S-M	•	•	•	•	Mild districts, no lime
Desfontainia spinosa	Sh	L.Sum		E	•			•				3/4	S-M	•	•	•	•	Mild districts
Drimys winteri	Sh T	Sp	•	E	•							½	M	•	•	•	•	
Elaeagnus x ebbingii vars	Sh	Aut	•	E	•	•					•	1	M	•	•	•	•	Seaside
Elaeagnus pungens vars	Sh	Aut	•	E	•	•						1	M	•	•	•	•	
Embothrium coccineum lanceolatum	T/Sh	L.Sp E.Sum		½E	•			•				3/4	M-L	•	•	•	•	No lime
Enkianthus campanulatus	Sh	L.Sp-E.Sum		D	•		••	•				1	M	•	•	•		No lime
Erica spp & vars: (many)	Sh	All year		E	•	•						1	S	•	•	•	•	
Escallonia spp & vars	Sh	Sum-E.Aut		E	•		••	•				3/4	L	•	•	•	•	Seaside
Eucalyptus, several spp	T	Time varies within spp		E	••	•		•	•	•		½, 3/4-1	M	•	•	•	•	Not coldest districts
Eucryphia 'Nymansay'	Sh	L.Sum-E.Aut		E	•			•				1	L	•	•	•	•	
Euonymus alatus	T	Insig		D			••	•	•	•	•	1	S	•	•	•		
Euonymus fortunei, some vars	Sh	Insig		E	••	••		•				1	S-M	•	•	•	•	
Fagus sylvatica 'Dawyck Purple'	T			D	•	••		•				1	L	•	•	•	•	
Fagus sylvatica 'Pendula'	T			D	••			••	•	•		1	M	•	•	•	•	
Fatsia japonica	Sh	Aut		E	••			•				3/4-1	M	•	•	•	•	
Fuchsia 'Riccartonii'	Sh	Sp-Aut		D	•	•		•				3/4	M-L	•	•	•	•	Mild districts
Garrya elliptica 'James Roof'	Sh	Winter		E	•							1	M	•		•	•	
Gleditsia triacanthos 'Ruby Lace'	T			D	•	••						1	M		•	•		
Gleditsia triacanthos 'Sunburst'	T			D	•	••						1	M		•	•		
Hamamelis mollis & vars	Sh	Wint	••	D	•		••					1	M			•	•	Flowers retained into winter
Hydrangea (Hortensias)	Sh	Sum-Aut		D	•			•				1	M		•	•		
Hydrangea (Lacecaps)	Sh	Sum-Aut		D	•			•				3/4-1	M		•	•		
Hydrangea 'Quadricolor'	Sh	Sum-Aut		D	•	••		•				3/4-1	M		•	•		
Hypericum 'Hidcote'	Sh	M.Sum-Aut		D	•			•				1	M		•	•		
Ilex (many)	T/Sh	Sum		E	••	•		•		•	••	1	M-L	•	•	•	•	
Lavandula angustifolia vars	Sh	Sum	••	E	•	•		•				1	S	•	•	•	•	
Lavatera 'Barnsley'	S-Sh	Sp-Aut			•							1	M	•	•	•		
Leucothöe fontansiana 'Rainbow'	Sh	Sp		E	•	••		•				1	S-M	•	•	•	•	No lime
Liriodendron tulipifera	T	Sum		D	•		•					1	VL	•	•	•		
Lithodora diffusa vars	Sh	Sum		E	•			•				1	S	•	•	•	•	No lime
Magnolia delavayi	T	Sum	•	E	••							3/4	L	•	•	•	•	Shelter
Magnolia grandiflora	T	Sum-E.Aut	•	E	••							3/4-1	M	•	•	•	•	Shelter
Magnolia globosa, sinensis, wilsonii	Sh T	E.Sum	••	D	•			•				3/4-1	L-M	•	•	•	•	M. wilsonii lime tolerant

TREES AND SHRUBS

	Tree or Shrub	Flowers	Scent	Evergreen or Deciduous	Foliage	Coloured Foliage	Autumn Colour	Shape	Bark (Stems)	Twigs (Branches)	Fruit	Hardiness	Size	Spring	Summer	Autumn	Winter	Comments
Mahonia japonica	Sh	L.Aut-E.Sp	•	E	•		•	•			•	1	M	•	•	•	•	
Mahonia x media vars	Sh	L.Aut-E.Sp	•	E	•			•			•	3/4-1	M	•	•	•	•	
Malus floribunda	T	Sp		D				•			•	1	M	•		•	•	Fruit into winter
Malus 'Profusion'	T	Sp		D	•	•				•	•	1	M	•	•	•	•	
Malus 'Red Jade'	T	Sp		D				•		•	•	1	S	•	•	•	•	Weeping
Myrtus luma	T/Sh	L.Sum-E.Aut		E	•				••	•		1/2-3/4	S L	•	•	•	•	Mild areas
Olearia macrodonta	Sh	Sum		E	•	•		•				3/4	L	•	•	•	•	Seaside
Osmanthus x burkwoodii	Sh	Sp	•	E	•							1	M	•	•	•	•	
Paeonia lutea ludlowii	Sh	L.Sp-E.Sum		E	•						•	1	M	•	•	•	•	
Paeonia suffruticosa vars	Sh	L.Sp-E.Sum		E	•						•	1	M	•	•	•	•	
Paulownia tomentosa (tree)	T	Sp		D	•				•			1	M-L	•	•			
Paulownia tomentosa (stooled)	Sh	—		D	••							1	M					
Pernettya mucronata vars	Sh	L.Sp-E.Sum		E	•			•			•	1	S	•	•	•	•	No lime
Photinia 'Red Robin'	Sh	—		E	•	•						1	M	•	•	•	•	
Photinia 'Redstart'	Sh	Sum		E	•	•					•	1	M	•	•	•	•	
Phygelius x rectus vars	S-Sh	Sum-Aut		E	•	•						1	M	•	•	•	•	
x Phylliopsis hillieri 'Pinocchio'	Sh	Sp & Aut		E	•	•						1	D	•	•	•	•	No lime
Pieris 'Bert Chandler'	Sh	No flower		E	••	••						3/4	M	•	•	•	•	No lime
Pieris 'Forest Flame'	Sh	Sp		E	••	••						1	M	•	•	•	•	No lime
Pieris 'Wakehurst'	Sh	Sp		E	••	••						3/4	M	•	•	•	•	No lime
Pieris japonica vars	Sh	Sp		E	••	••						3/4-1	S-M	•	•	•	•	No lime
Pittosporum 'Garnettii'	Sh	Sp	•	E	•	•		•		•		3/4	S-M	•	•	•	•	Mild areas
Prunus cerasifera 'Pissardii'	T	Sp		D	•	•	•					1	M	•	•	•	•	
Prunus incisa 'Praecox'	T/Sh	Winter		D	•	•	•					1	M	•	•	•	•	
Prunus sargentii	T	E.Sp		D	•	•	•	•	•			1	M	•	•	•	•	
Prunus serrula	T	Sp		D	•				•			1	M	•	•	•	•	
Pyracantha (several)	Sh	Sp-E.Sum		E	•	•					••	1	M	•	•	•	•	
Pyrus salicifolia 'Pendula'	T	Sp		D	•	•		•		•	•	1	M	•	•	•	•	
Quercus macranthera	T			D	•	•				•		1	M	•	•	•	•	
Quercus robur 'Concordia'	T			D	•	•		•				1	S	•	•	•	•	
Quercus suber	T			E	•				••			3/4	M	•	•	•	•	Shelter in cold areas
Rhamnus alaternus 'Argenteovariegata'	Sh			E	•	•						3/4	M	•	•	•	•	Shelter in cold areas

TREES AND SHRUBS

Rhododendron

Scent: Albatross group, *auriculatum*, 'Countess of Haddingdon', *decorum*, 'Fragrantissimum'***, 'Loderi' vars, 'Lady Alice' Fitzwilliam'*, *luteum* (syn. *Azalea pontica*).
Deciduous azaleas: Ghent, occidentale and rustica hybrids.

Outstanding foliage: *macabeanum**, *sinogrande**, *falconeri*, *arboreum* forms*, *yakushimanum**, 'May Day' and many others

Bark: *thomsonii*, 'Cornish Cross'**

Autumn foliage: deciduous azaleas

** Hardiness = 1/2
* Hardiness = 3/4

	Tree or Shrub	Scent	Flowers	Evergreen or Deciduous	Foliage	Coloured Foliage	Autumn Colour	Shape	Bark (Stems)	Twigs (Branches)	Fruit	Hardiness	Size	Spring	Summer	Autumn	Winter	Comments
Rhus typhina 'Dissecta'	T·Sh		E.Sum	D	●	●	●	●	●	●	●	1	M	●	●	●	●	
Robinia pseudoacacia 'Frisia'	T		—	D	●	●	●					1	M	●	●	●		
Romneya coulteri	S·Sh	●	M.Sum-M.Aut	D		●				●		1	S-M	●	●	●		
Rosa			*Too many to list – see Chapter 6 for a selection*															
Rubus cockburnianus	Sh		Insig	D	●	●			●		●	1	M	●			●	
Ruta graveolens 'Jackman's Blue'	Sh		Sum	E	●	●		●				1	S	●		●	●	
Salix caprea 'Kilmarnock'	T		L.Wint	D	●			●●		●		1	S	●	●	●	●	
Salix daphnoides	T		Sp	D					●	●		1	S	●	●	●	●	
Salix irrorata	Sh		Sp	D					●	●		1	M	●	●	●	●	
Salix magnifica	T·Sh		Sp	D	●							1	S-M	●	●	●		
Sambucus racemosa 'Plumosa Aurea'	Sh	●●	Sp	D	●	●					●	1	M-L	●	●	●		
Sarcococca hookeriana	Sh	●●	Wint	E	●						●	1	S			●	●	
Skimmia japonica reevesiana	Sh	●	Sp	E	●			●			●●	1	D-S	●	●	●	●	Hermaphrodite: needs a mate for fruit
Skimmia japonica 'Veitchii' and 'Foremanii'	Sh	●	Sp	E	●●			●●			●●	1	S	●	●	●	●	
Sorbus cashmiriana	T		Sp	D	●		●●				●	1	S	●	●	●	●	Fruits persistent
Sorbus hupehensis	T		Sp	D	●		●●				●●	1	S	●	●	●	●	Fruit persistent
Sorbus 'Joseph Rock'	T		Sp	D	●		●	●			●	1	M	●	●	●	●	
Sorbus x thibetica 'John Mitchell'	T		Insig	D	●●							1	M-L	●	●			
Stuartia pseudocamellia	T		L.Sum	D	●		●	●●	●			1	S-M	●	●	●	●	No lime
Trachycarpus fortunei	T		E.Sum	E	●			●	●		●	1	M	●	●	●	●	Shelter from strong winds
Viburnum x bodnantense vars	Sh	●●	Wint	D	●							1	M	●			●	
Viburnum x burkwoodii	Sh	●●	L.Wint-E.Sp	E	●							1	M	●			●	
Viburnum carlesii vars	Sh	●●	Sp	D	●						●	1	M		●	●		
Viburnum plicatum 'Mariesii'	Sh		L.Sp-E.Sum	D	●		●	●●				1	M	●	●	●	●	
Yucca gloriosa 'Variegata'	T		L.Sum-E.Aut	E	●	●●		●		●		3/4	S-M	●	●	●	●	No lime
Yucca recurvifolia	T		L.Sum	E	●							1	S	●	-	●	●	No lime
Zenobia pulverulenta	Sh	●	Sum	E	●	●		●		●		1	S	●	●	●	●	No lime

CLIMBERS

	Flowers	Scent	Evergreen or Deciduous	Foliage	Coloured Foliage	Autumn Colour	Fruit	Hardiness	Height m (ft)	Spring	Summer	Autumn	Winter	Comments
Actinidia kolomikta	Sum	•	D	•	••		see note	1	5 (15)	•	•	•	•	Edible fruit, but male plants only available
Akebia quinata	Sp	•	D	•			•	1	10 (30)	•	•	•		
Berberidopsis corallina	L.Sum		E	•				3/4	5 (15)	•	•			Shade
Campsis x tagliabuana 'Mme. Galen'	L.Sum		D	•				1	10 (30)	•	•			Full sun
Clematis alpina 'Frances Rivis'	Sp	•	D	•				1	2.5 (8)	•				
Clematis armandii	Sp	•	E	•				3/4	5 (15)	•	•	•		Sun
Clematis cirrhosa balearica	Wint		E	•			seed heads	1	4 (13)	•	•	•	•	
Clematis montana vars	Sp	•	D	•				1	7 (23)	•	•			
Clematis: Large-flowered hybs.														There are a great many large-flowered hybrids. Flowering, according to variety, occurs during the following periods: late spring and early summer; midsummer to early autumn; late spring to early summer and then again in early autumn. Those in the first group should be pruned by cutting back the old flowering growths as soon as flowering is over. The rest should be hard pruned to within 30cm (1ft) of ground level in late winter or early spring. All are fully hardy.
Hedera (many)	Insig		E	••	••			3/4-1	various	•	•	•	•	
Hydrangea petiolaris	Sum		D	•				1	20 (60)	•	•			
Jasminum officinale	E.Sum to E.Aut	••	D	•				3/4	6 (20)	•	•	•		
Jasminum x stephanense	Sum	••	D	•	•			3/4-1	7 (23)	•	•	•		
Lapageria rosea	Sum & Aut		E	•				1/2	4 (13)	•	•	•		Shade. Mild areas
Lonicera caprifolium	Sum	••	D	•			•	1	6 (20)	•	•	•	•	Non-strangling
Mandevilla laxa (syn *M. suaveolens*)	Sum-E.Aut	••	D	•				1/2	5 (15)	•	•	•		Mildest areas
Parthenocissus quinquefolia	Insig		D	•		••	•	1	20 (60)	•	•	•		
Solanum crispum 'Glasnevin'	M.Sum-M.Aut	•	D	•				1	5 (15)	•	•	•		
Vitis 'Brant'	Insig		D	•		•	••	1	8 (26)	•	•	•		Edible grapes
Vitis coignetiae	Insig		D	•		••	•	1	15 (45)		•	•		
Wisteria floribunda forma macrobotrys 'Multijuga'	L.Sp-E.Sum	•	D	•				1	5 (15)	•	•			Racemes to 1m (3ft)

BIBLIOGRAPHY

The best way to become acquainted
with a subject is to write a book about it.

DISRAELI

Austin, David. *The Heritage of the Rose* (Antique Collectors' Club, 1990)

Bean, W.J. *Trees and Shrubs Hardy in the British Isles* (John Murray, 1976; supplement 1988)

Hillier Nurseries (Winchester) Ltd. *The Hillier Manual of Trees & Shrubs* (David & Charles, 1991)

Hobhouse, Penelope. *Colour in Your Garden* (Frances Lincoln, 1985)

Jekyll, Gertrude. *Colour Schemes for the Flower Garden* (8th edition, 1936, revised and reprinted by Windward/Frances Lincoln, 1987)

Kelly, John. *Ferns in Your Garden* (Souvenir Press, 1991)

Mathew, B. *Dwarf Bulbs* (Batsford, 1974)

Midgley, K. *Garden Design* (Penguin, 1967)

Page, Russell. *The Education of a Gardener* (Penguin, 1985)

Philip, C. *The Plant Finder* (Headmain, 1991 et seq.)

Synge, P.M. *Collins Guide to Bulbs* (Collins, 1961)

Thomas, G.S. *Perennial Garden Plants* (Dent, 1990)

ACKNOWLEDGEMENTS

The author and publishers would like to thank the following for their invaluable help in providing the photographs reproduced in this book:

David Austin Roses: pp1, 115

Linda Clements: p100

John Glover: pp39, 69, 77, 101, 102, 104, 108, 110-11, 115

Clive Nichols: pp 2-3, 4-5, 20-1, 26, 29, 31, 34-5, 41, 60-1, 83, 84, 87, 90, 91, 92-3, 113, 119, 120-1, 128, 131

All other photographs by the author and Nicola Kelly.

Photographic locations, where known, are listed below:

David Austin Roses, Albrighton, Wolverhampton: pp1, 115; Picton Garden, Malvern, Hereford and Worcester: pp4-5, 90; Kells House, Kells Bay, Co. Kerry: p6; Anne's Grove, Castle-townroche, Co. Cork: pp8 (top), 52 (top); Royal Horticultural Society Gardens, Rosemoor, Devon: pp8 (lower), 23; Chilcombe House, Chilcombe, Dorchester, Dorset: p11; West Barn Abbotsbury Gardens, Dorset: pp11 (lower), 22, 38, 39 (top), 44, 46, 50 (top), 52 (lower), 65, 72, 75 (lower); The Weald, East Portlemouth, Devon: p14; Dunloe Castle Hotel, Killarney, Co. Kerry: p16; The Beth Chatto Garden, Elmstead Market, Colchester, Essex: pp17, 33, 123; Mount Usher, Co. Wicklow: p17; Saville Garden, Windsor Great Park, Berks: pp18, 51 (lower), 68, 71, 77, 107; Lower Hall, Shropshire: pp20-1, 31, 70, 113; Coates Manor Garden, Sussex: p26; Royal Horticultural Society Gardens, Wisley, Surrey: p27, 50 (lower), 76, 78 (right), 94, 105, 118; Chenies Manor House, Bucks: pp29, 60-1, 191; Lower House Farm, Gwent, Wales: pp34-5; The National Trust, Killerton, Devon: p40; Tilgates Garden, Bletchingley, Surrey: p41; Muckross House, Killarney, Co. Kerry: pp49, 99; The Manor House, Abbotsbury, Dorset: p51 (top); Pound Hill, Sussex: p53; University Botanic Garden, Leiden, Holland: pp54, 126; West Street, Abbotsbury, Dorset: p58; Barnsdale, Oakham, Rutland: p67; Bramble Cottage, Ottery St Mary, Devon: p75 (top); Spinners, Boldre, Hampshire: p78 (left); The National Trust, Overbecks, Sharpitor, Devon: p81; Jenkyn Place Garden, Hampshire: p83; The Priory, Kemerton, Hereford and Worcester: p84; Blarney House, Blarney, Co. Cork: p87; Dartington Hall Garden, Devon: p92-3; Bridgemont, Totnes, Devon: p100; Vatican Garden, Vatican City, Rome: p117; Mill Court Garden, Hampshire: p119; Brook Cottage, Oxfordshire: p120-1; Barnsley House, Gloucestershire: p128

INDEX OF PLANTS

Numbers in italics denote illustrations

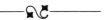